Awesome Dinosaurs

A Children's Coloring Book

ISBN-13: 978-1544289427
ISBN-10: 1544289421

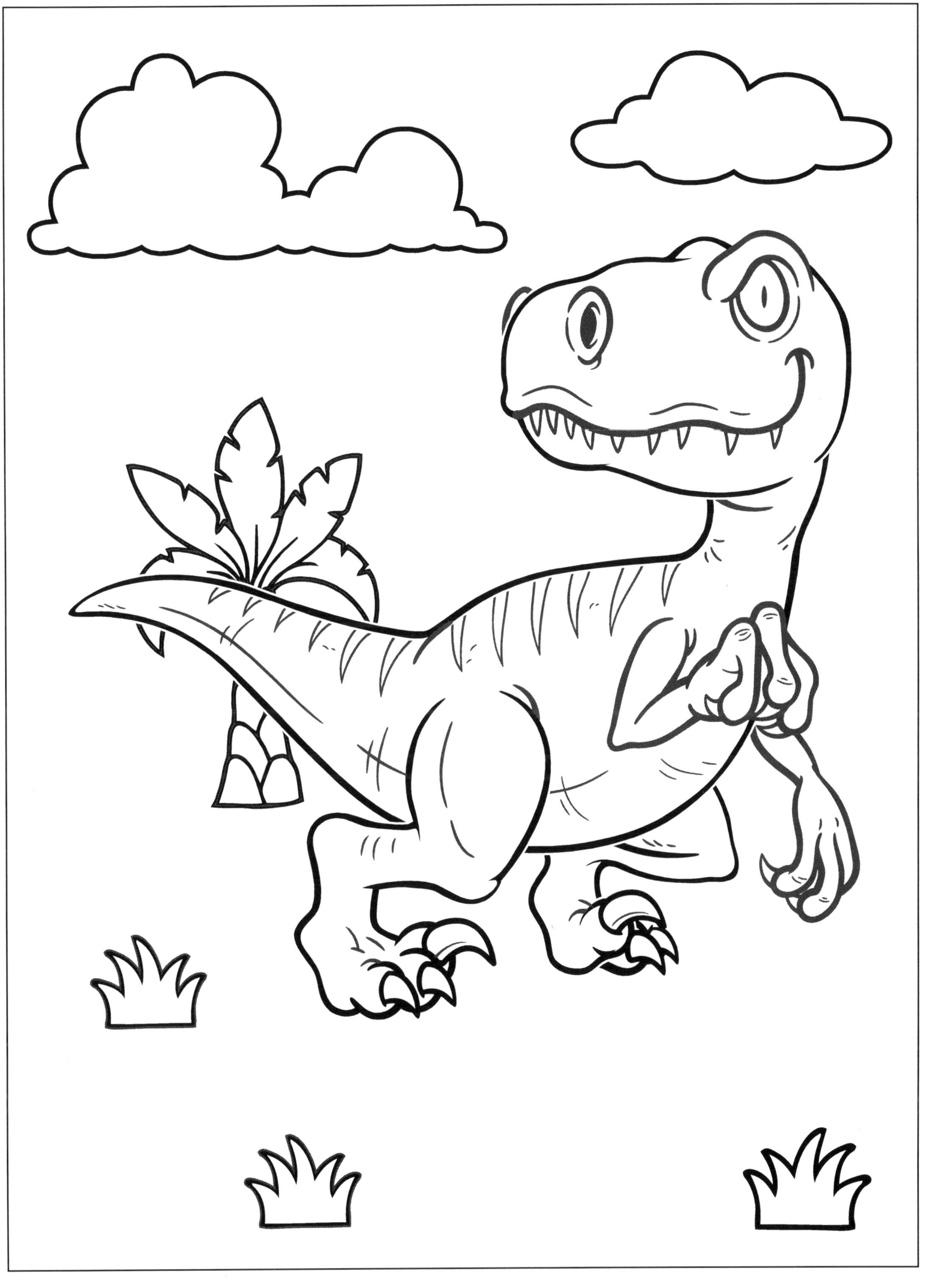

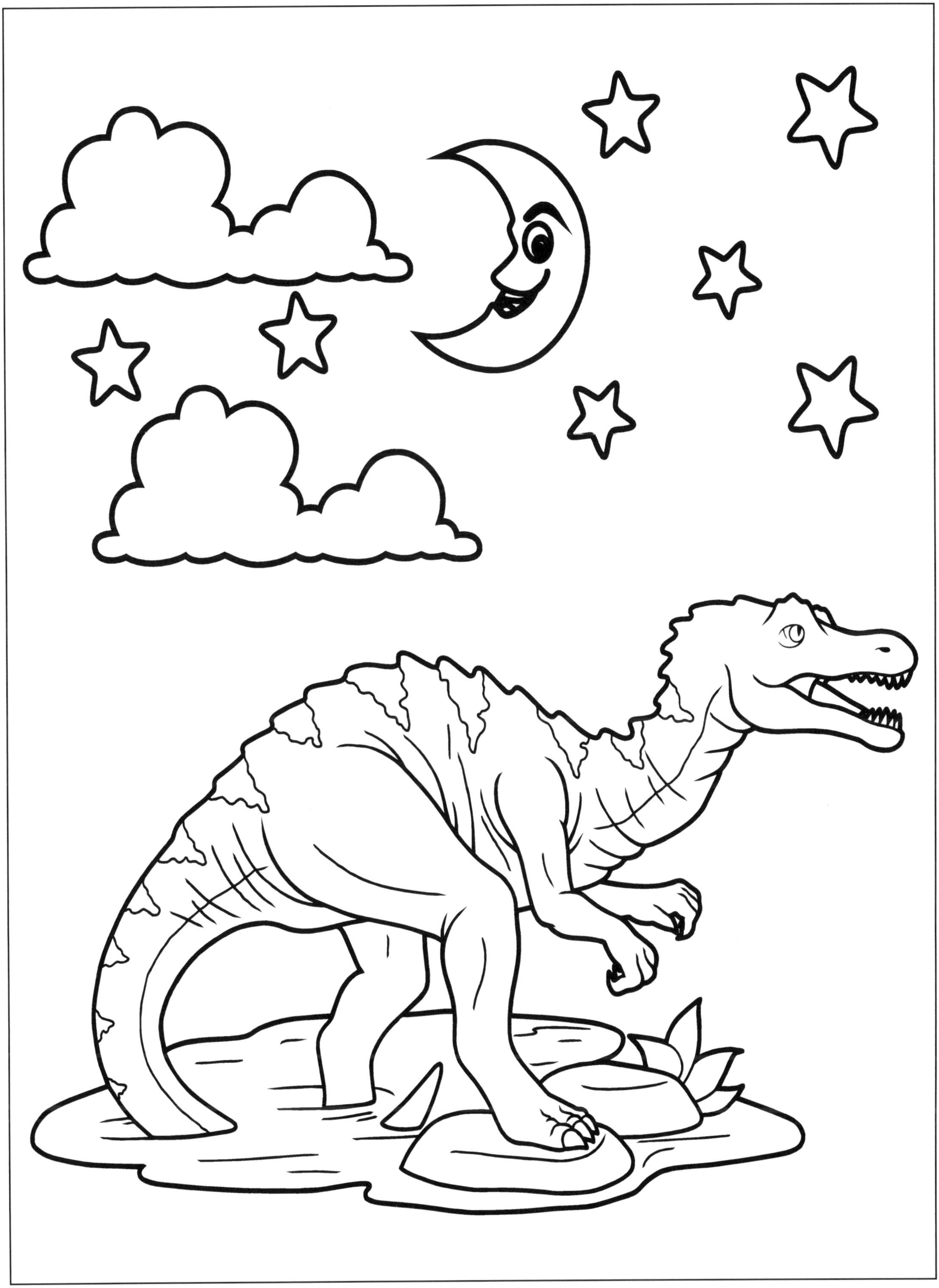

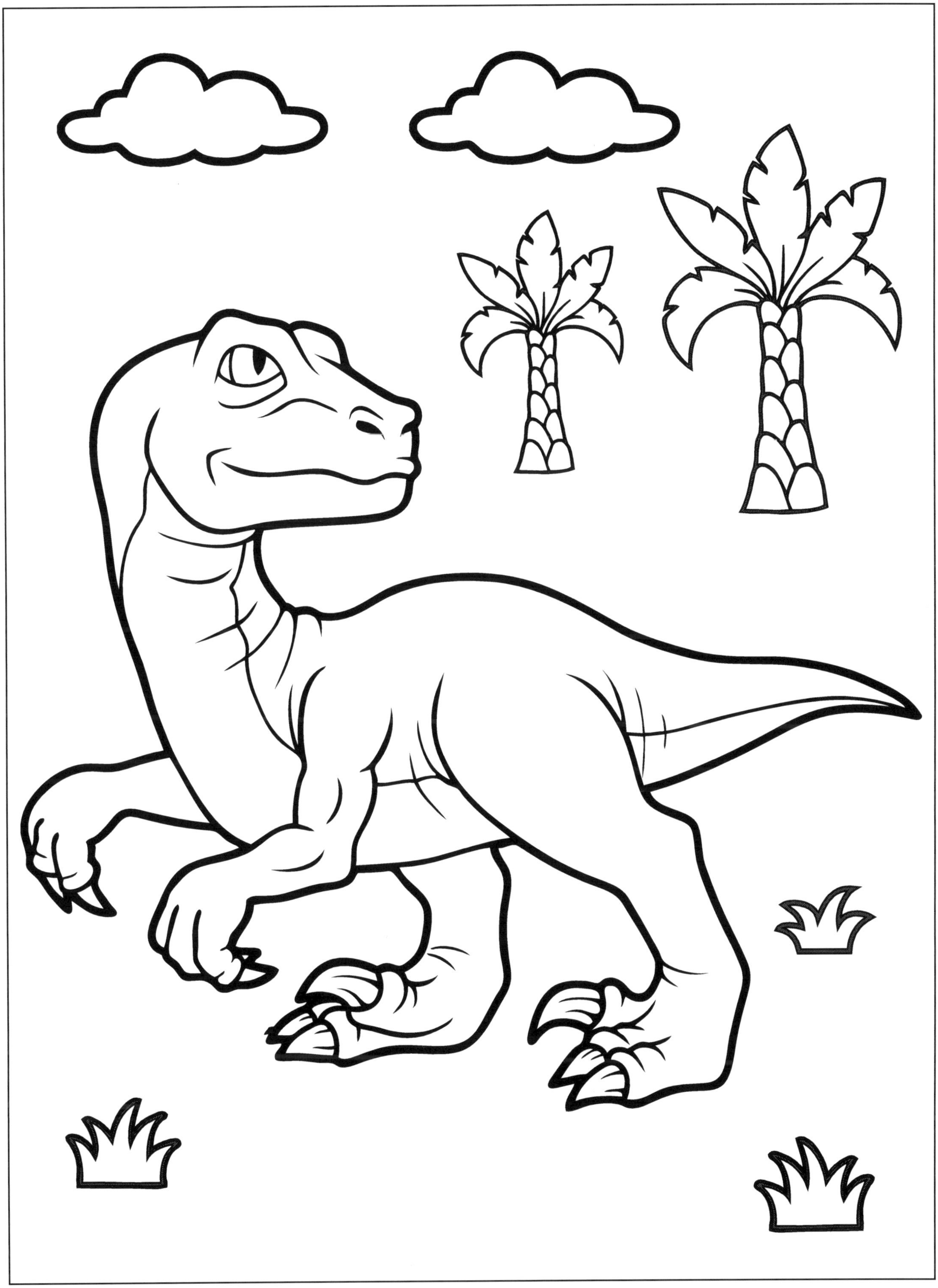

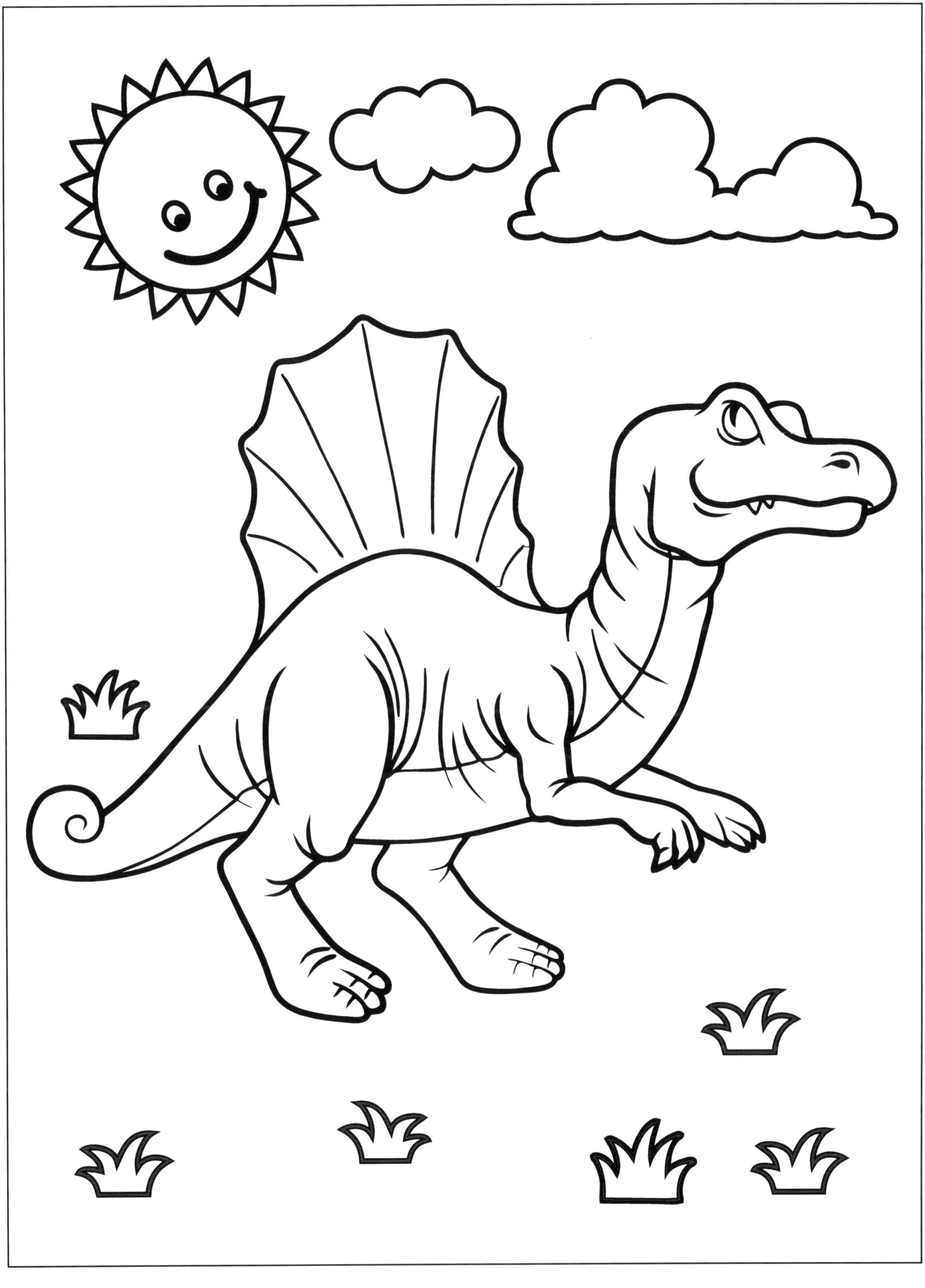

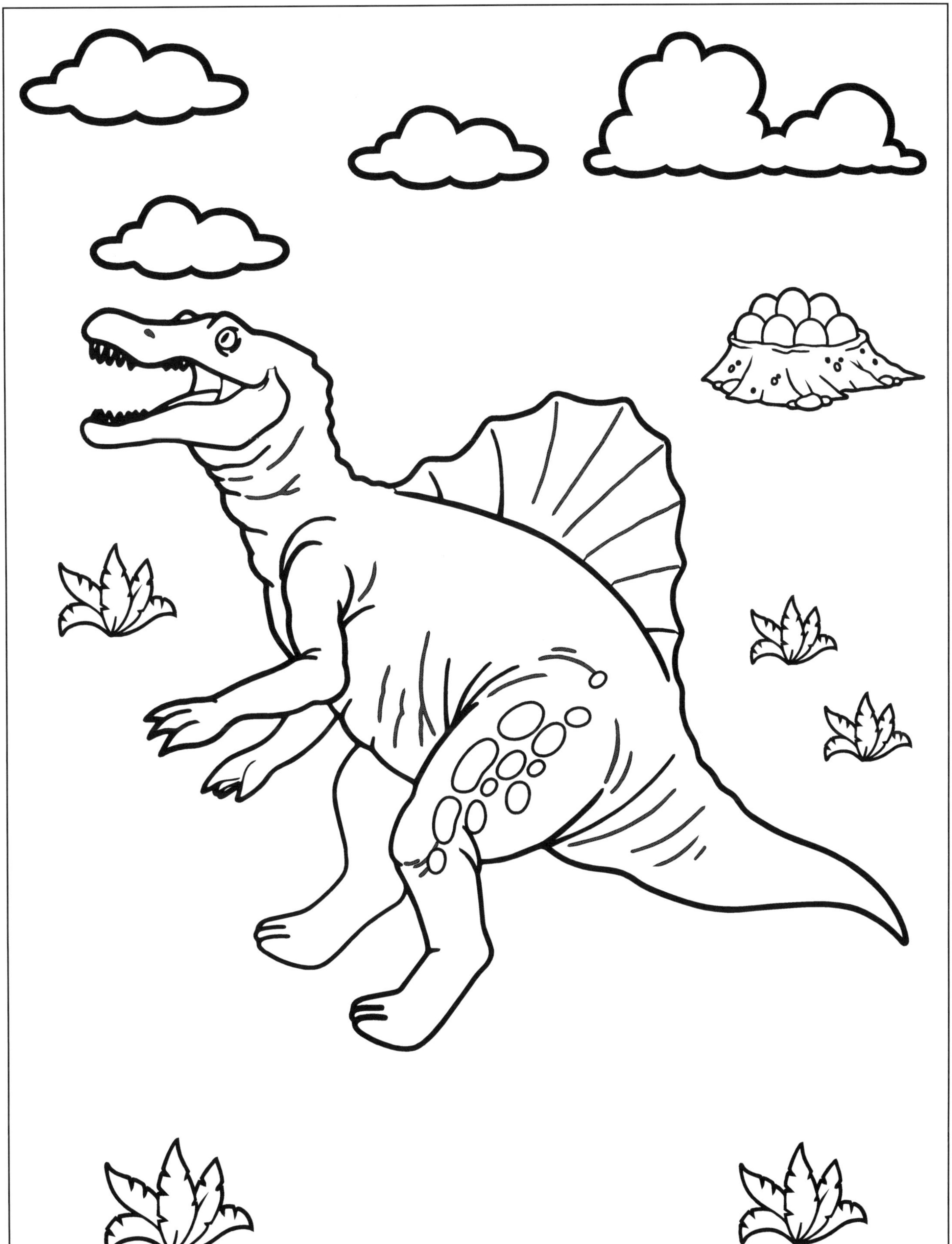

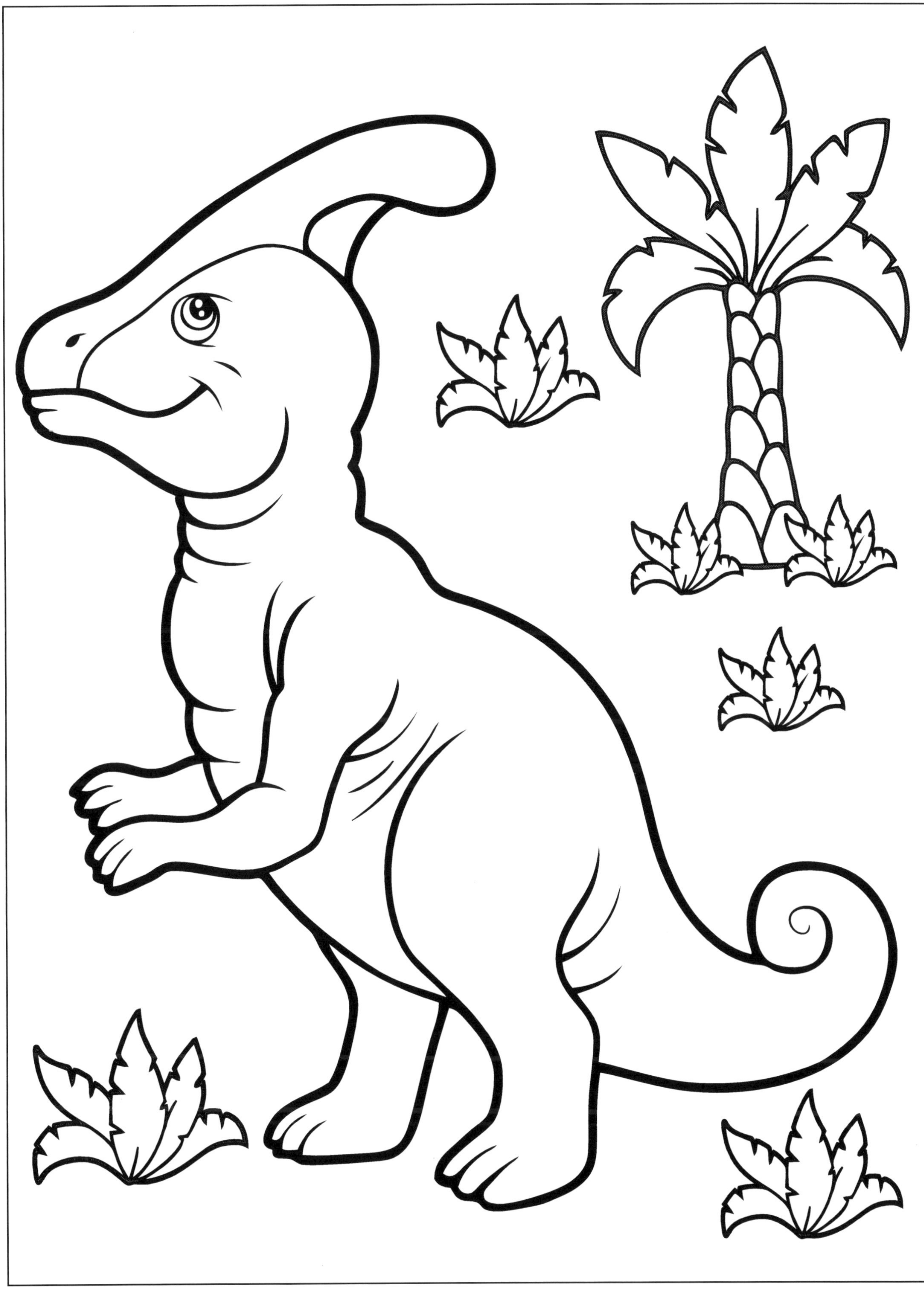

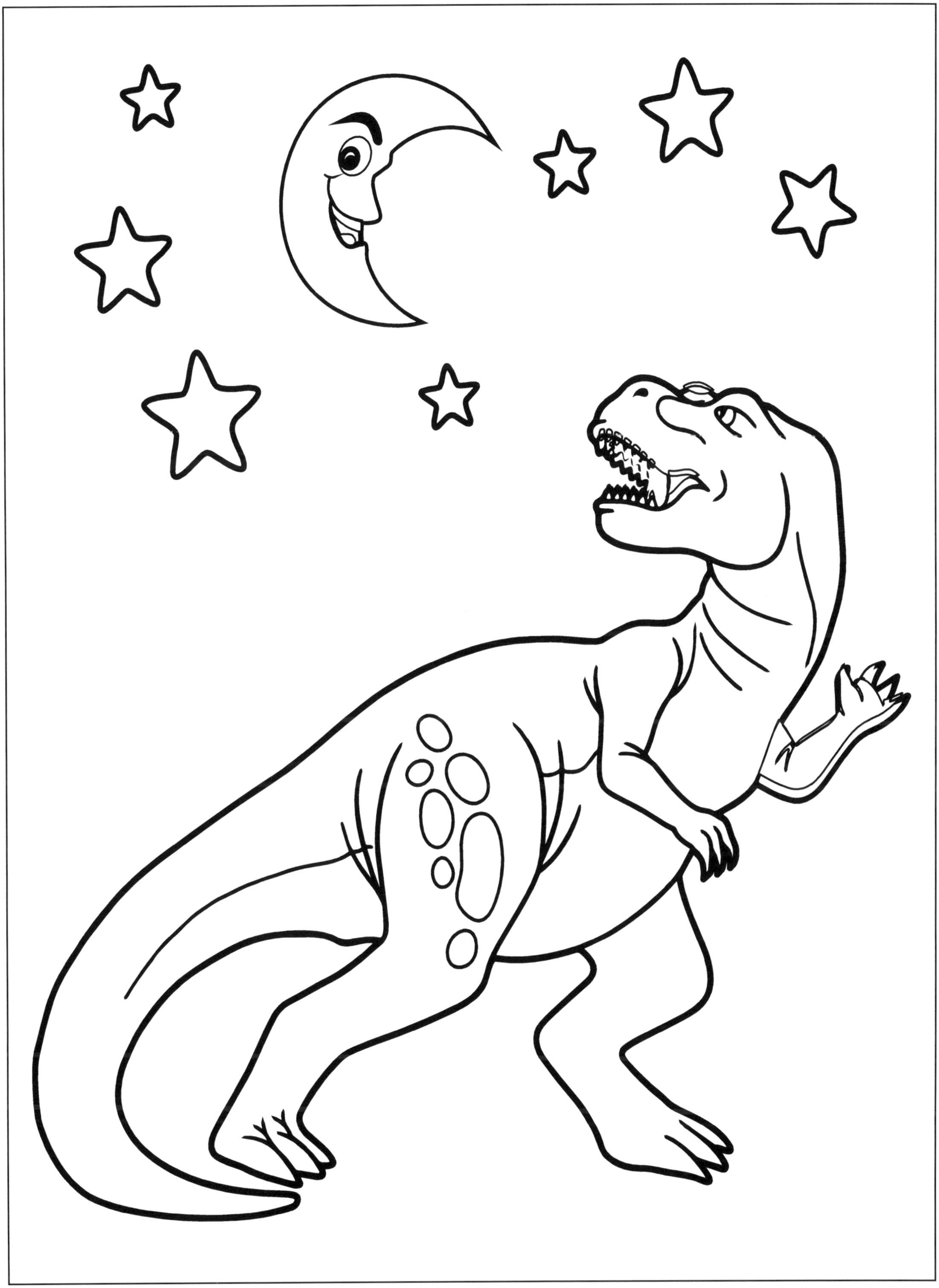

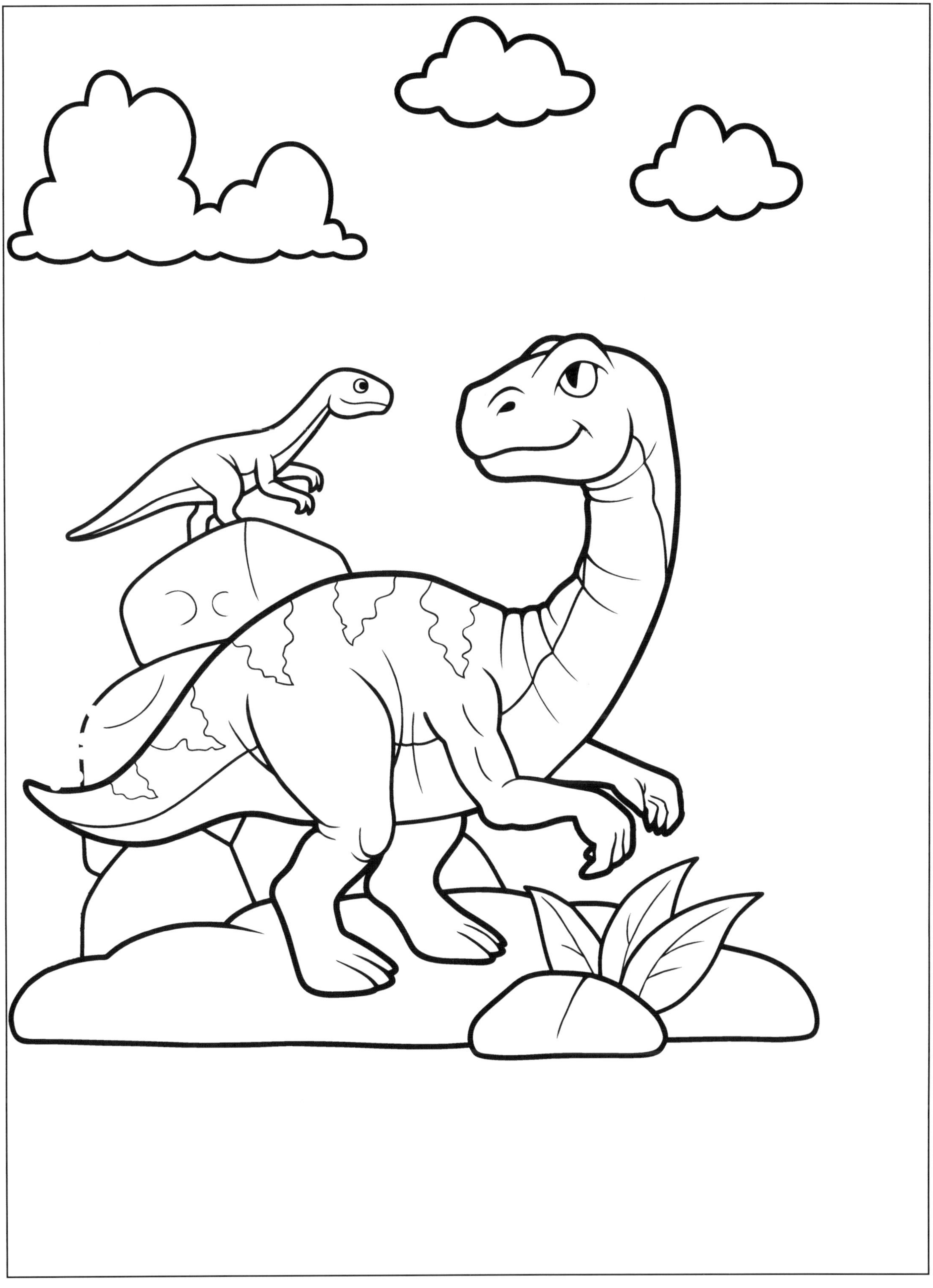

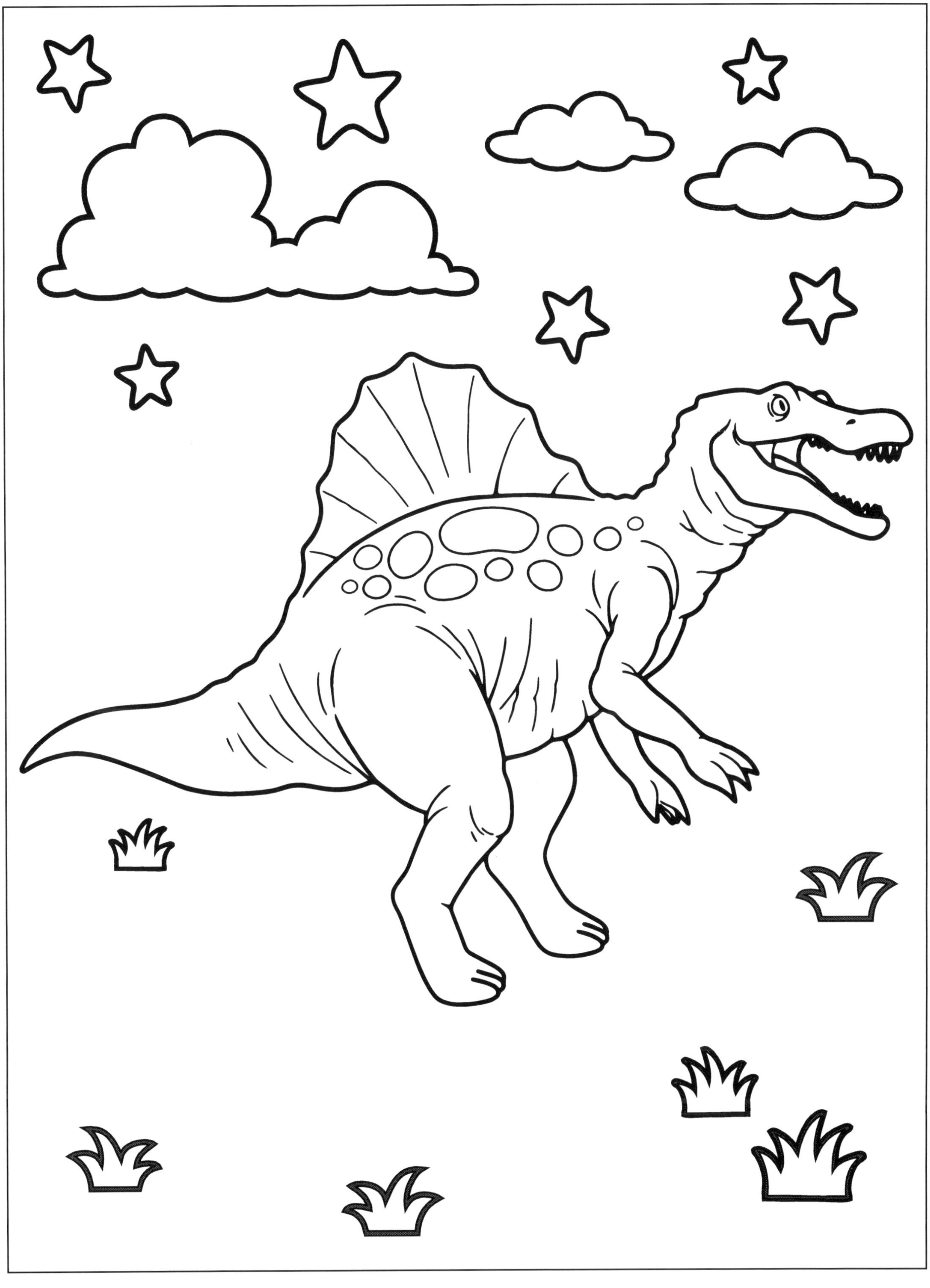

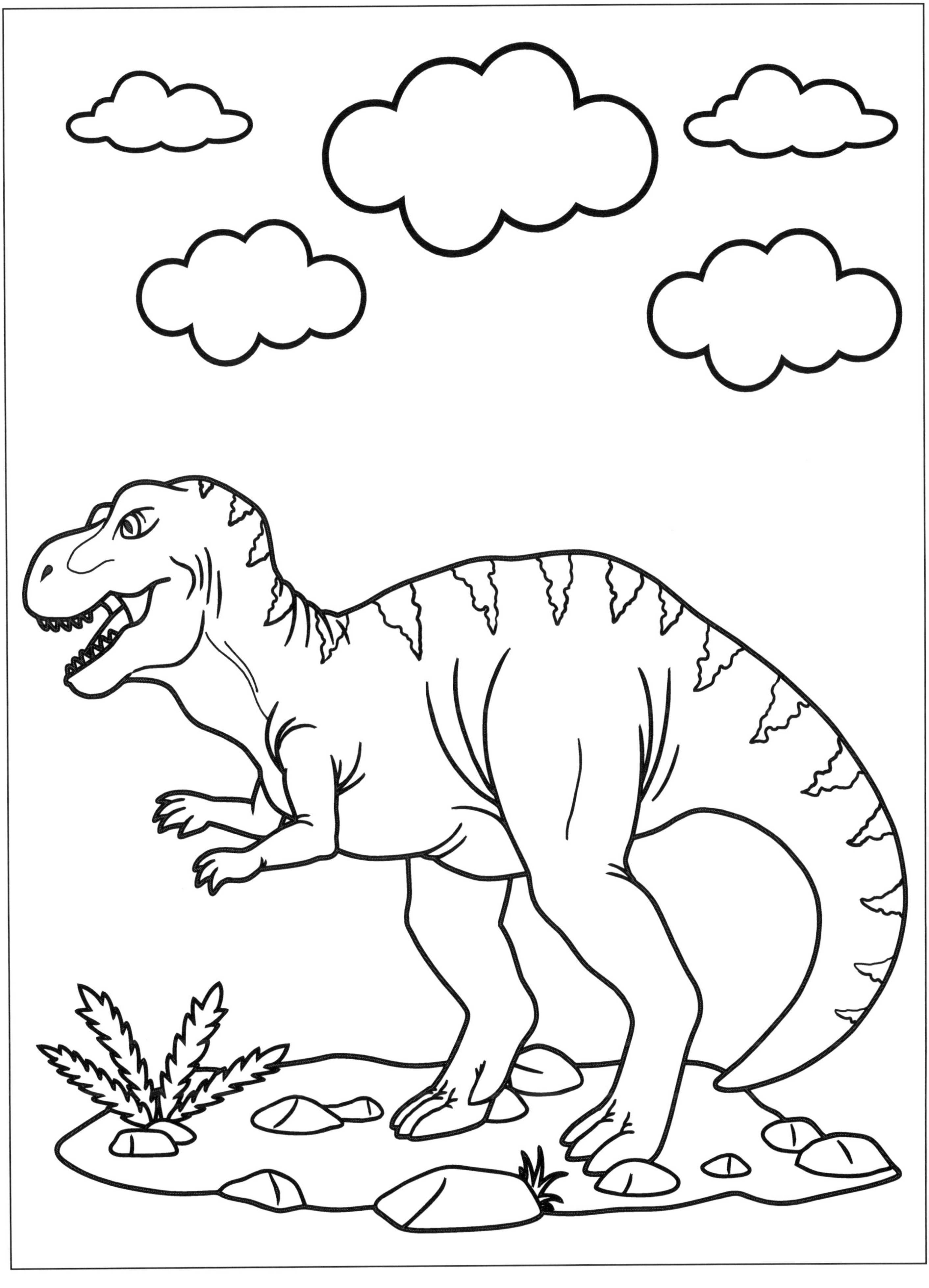

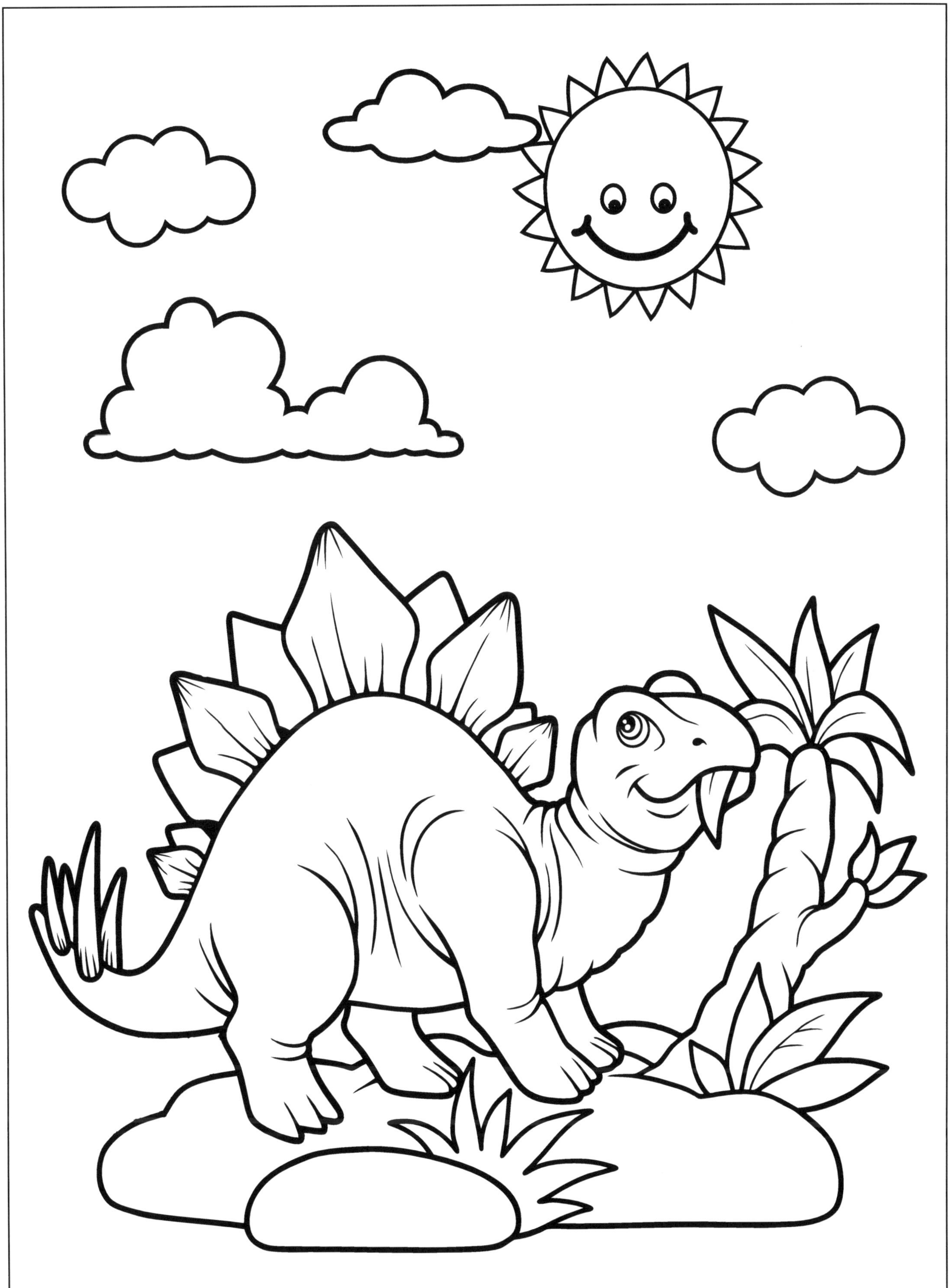

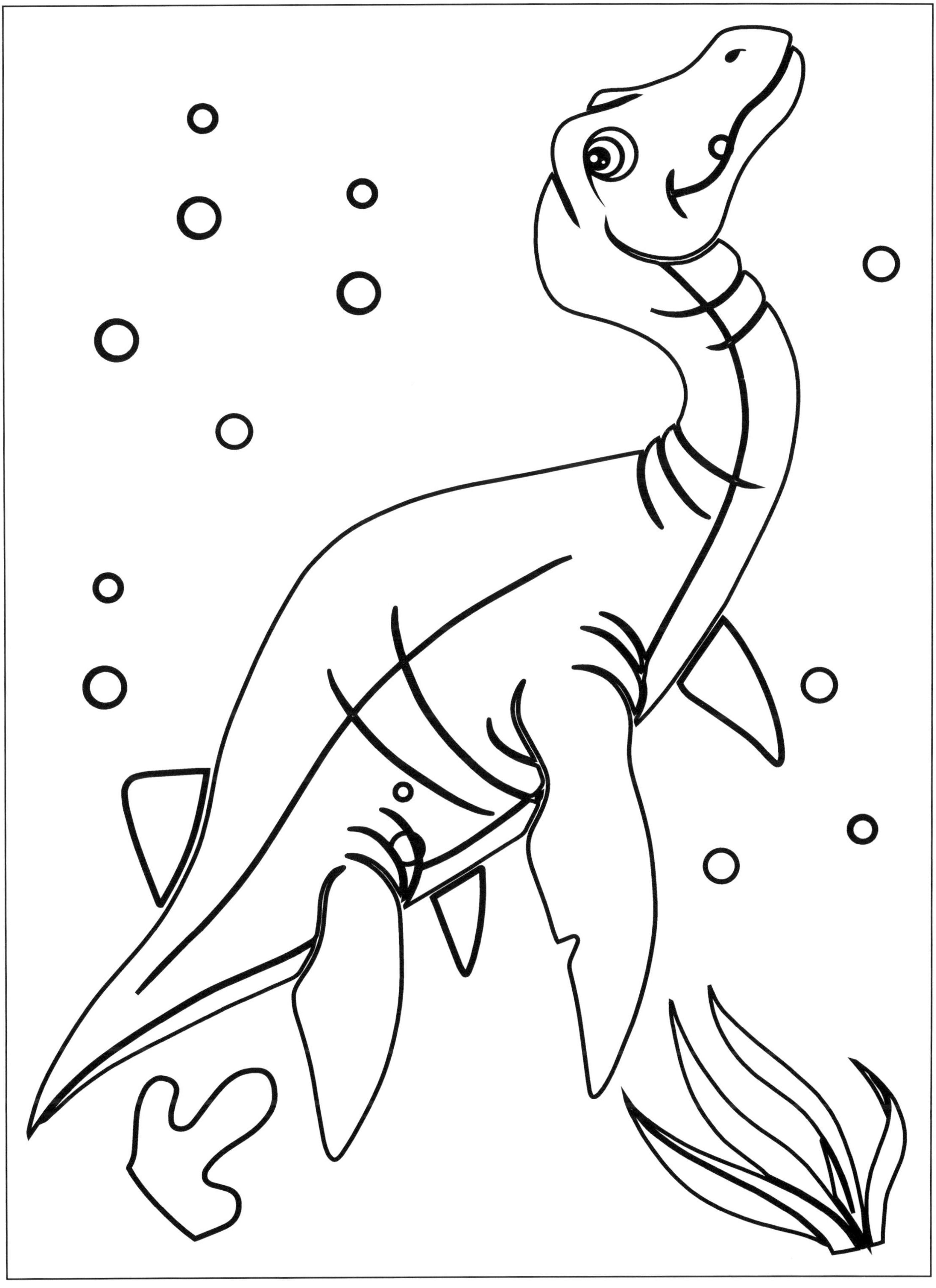

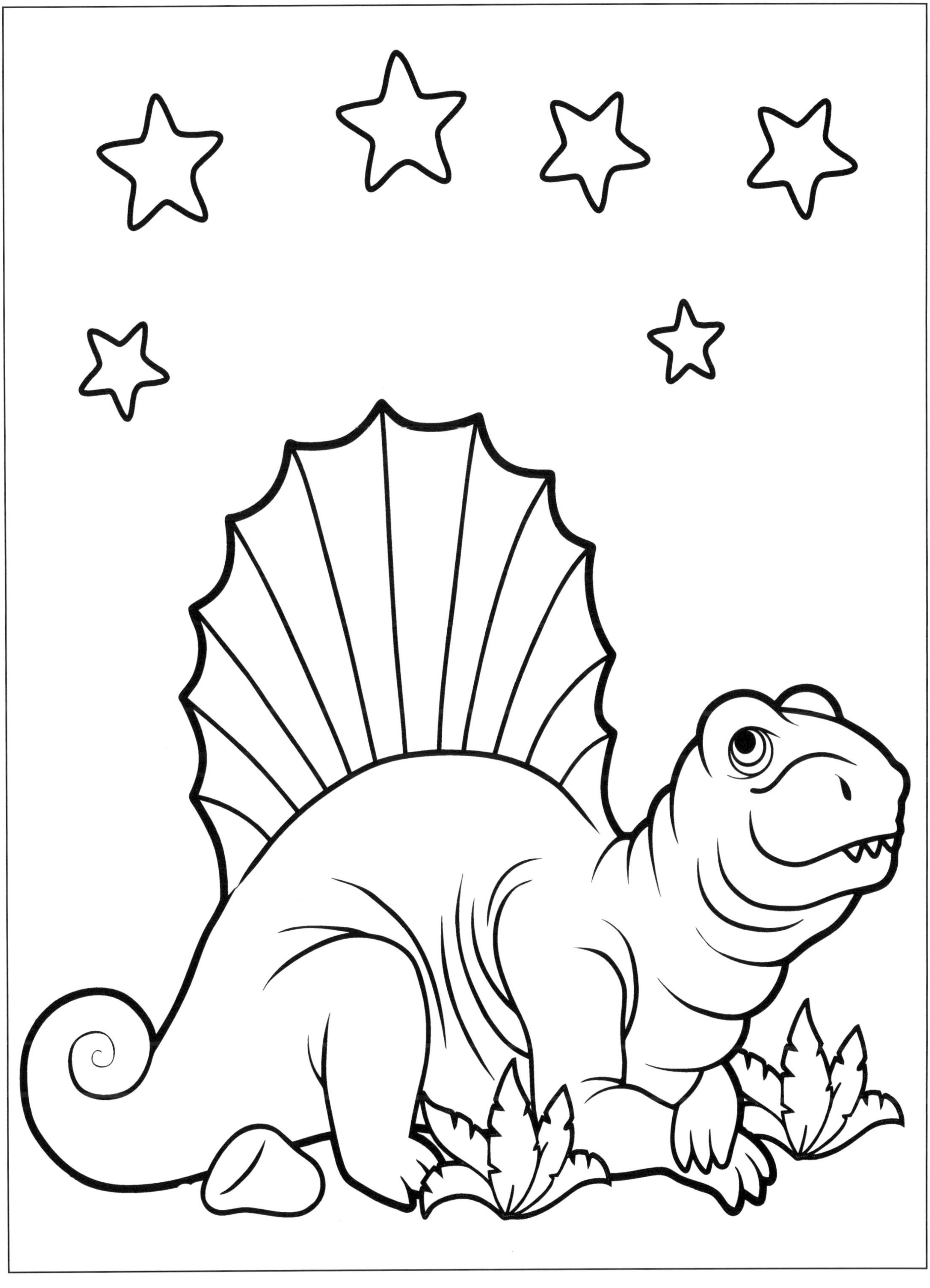

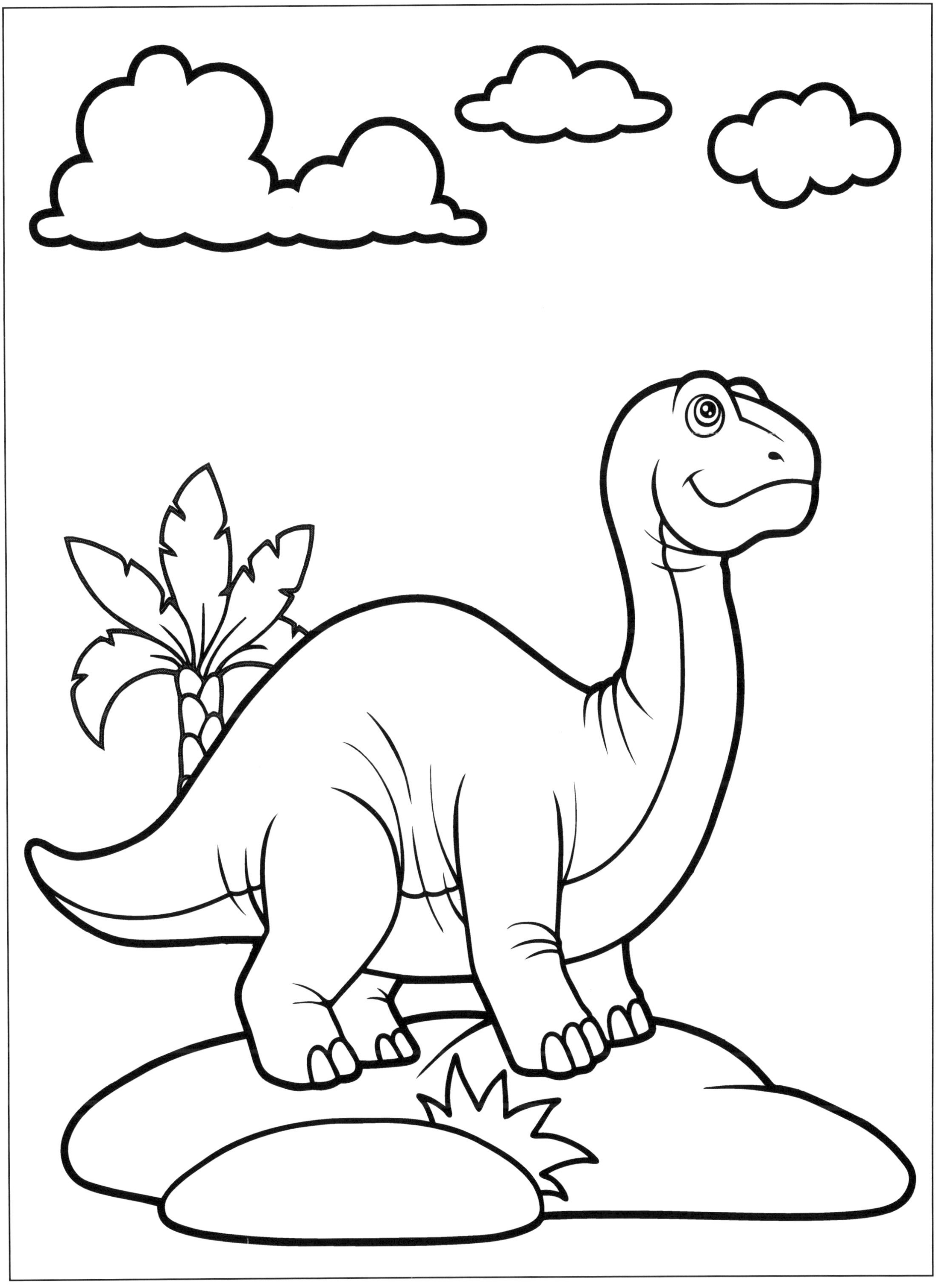

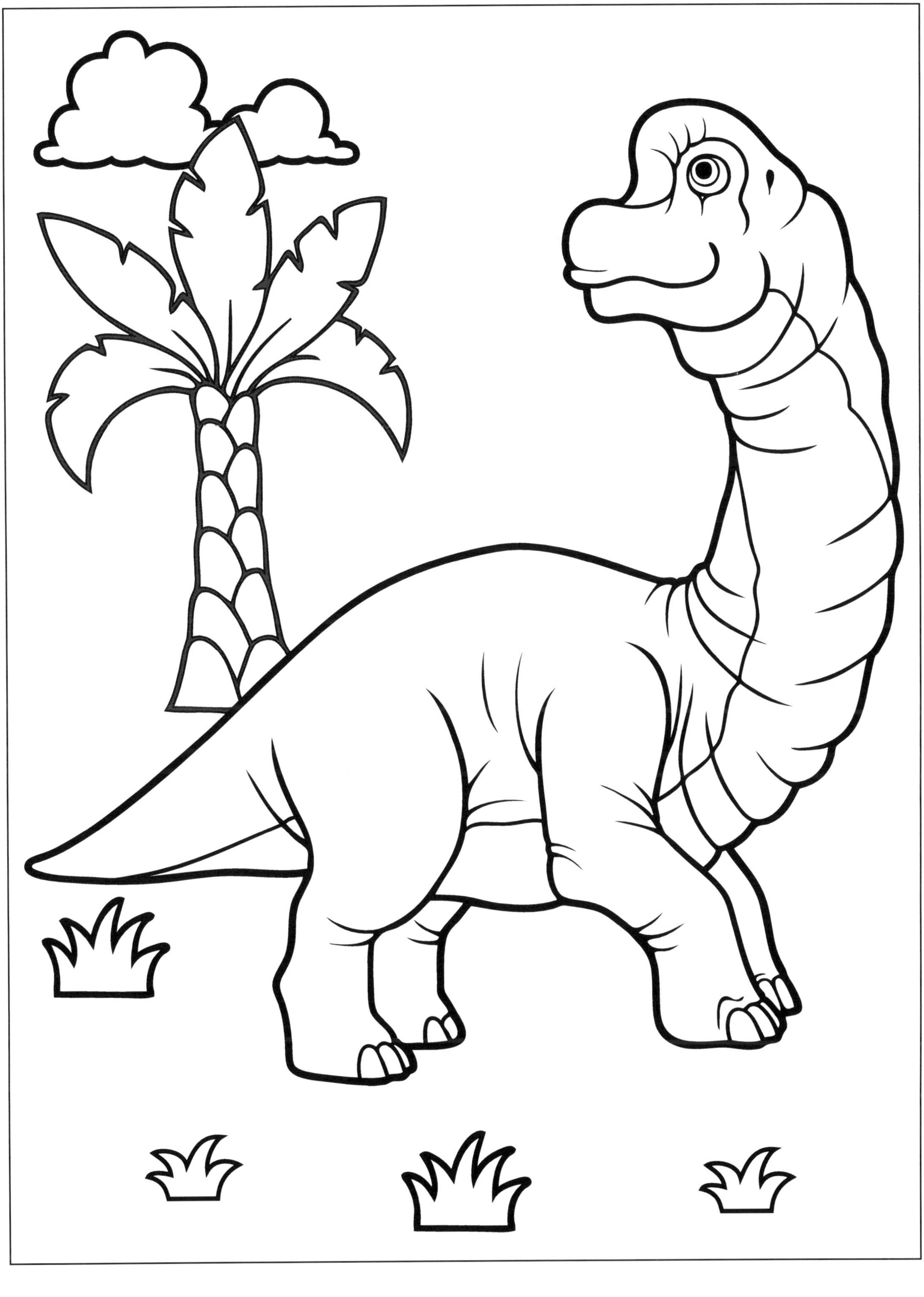

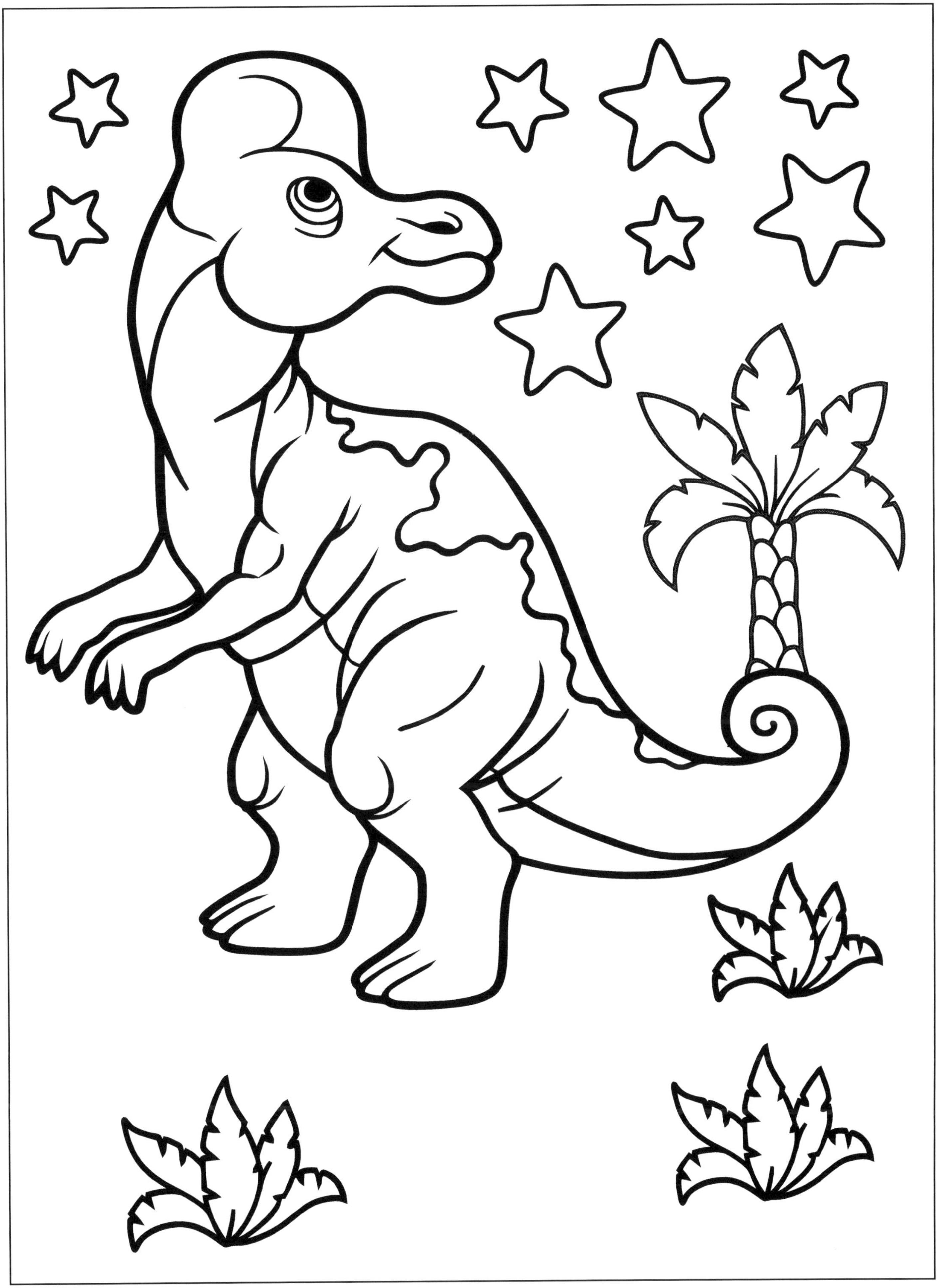

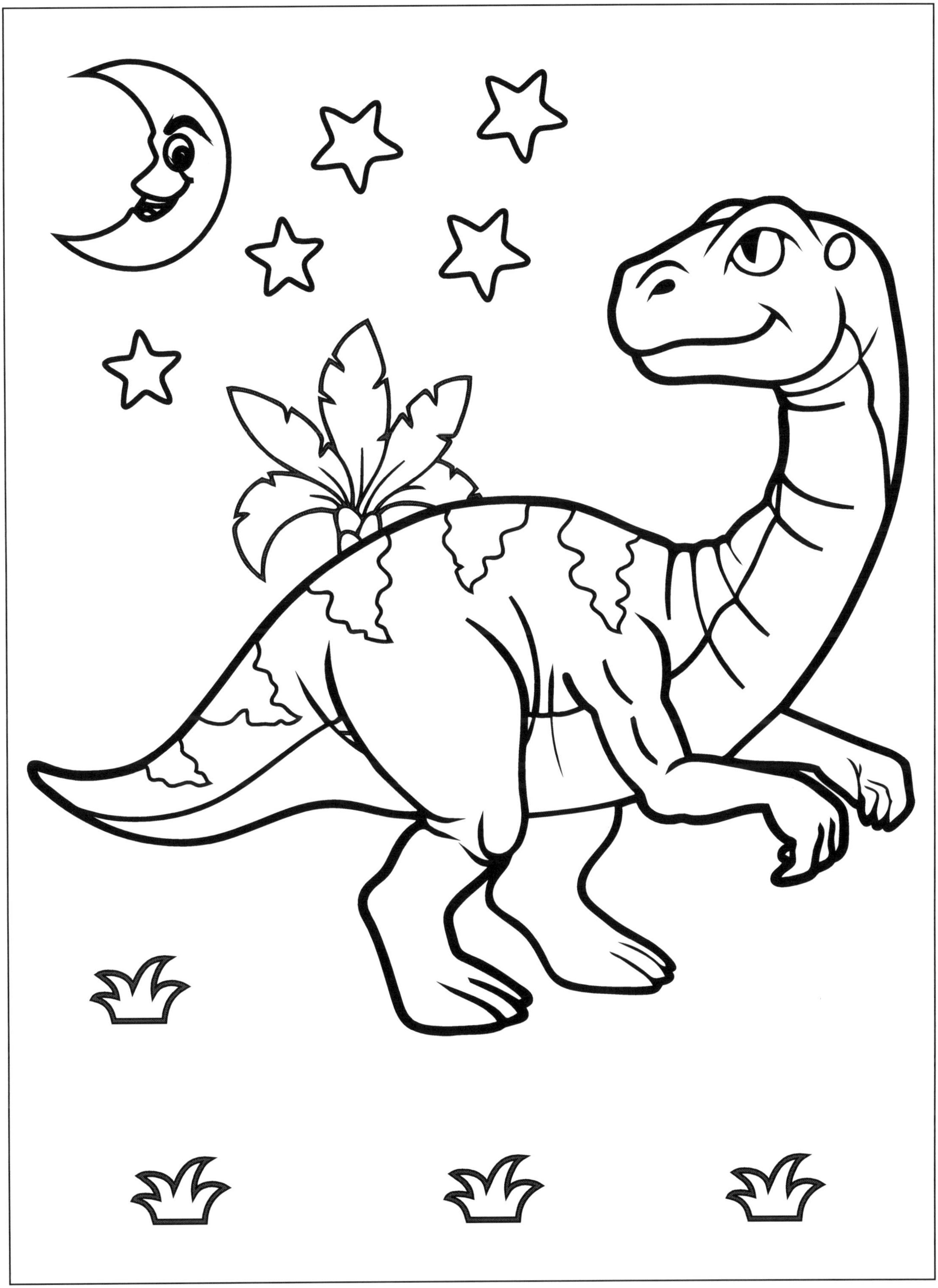

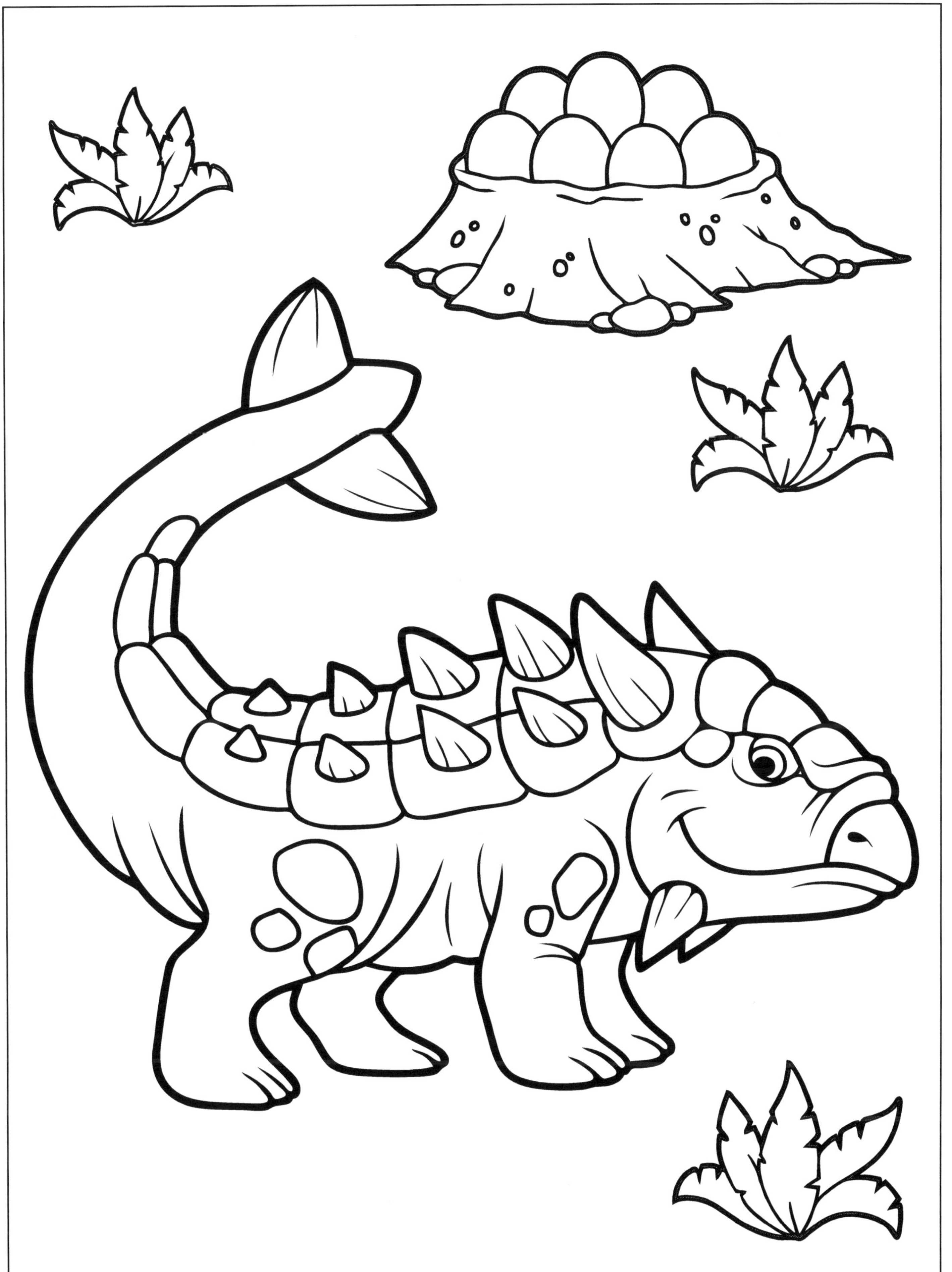

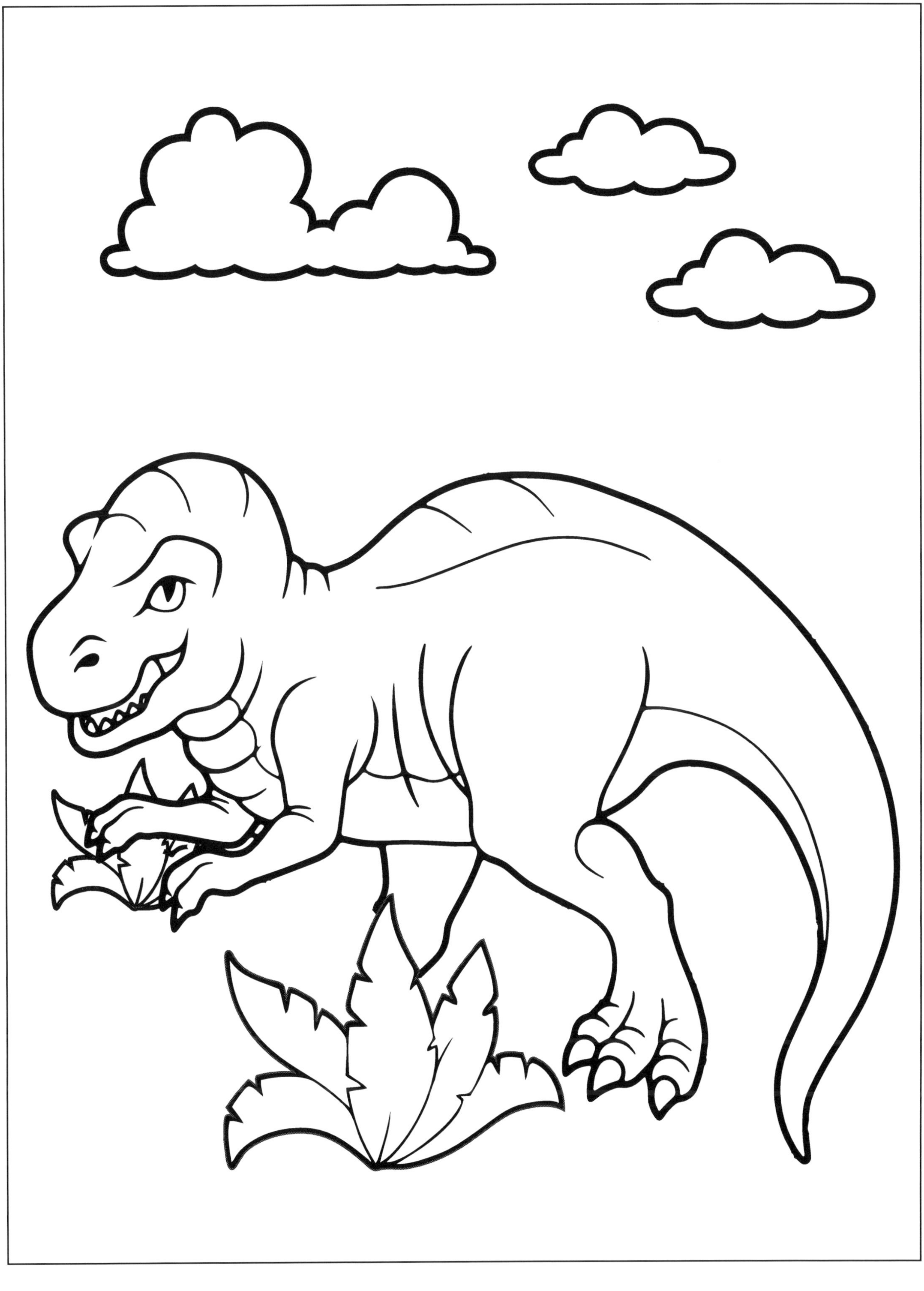

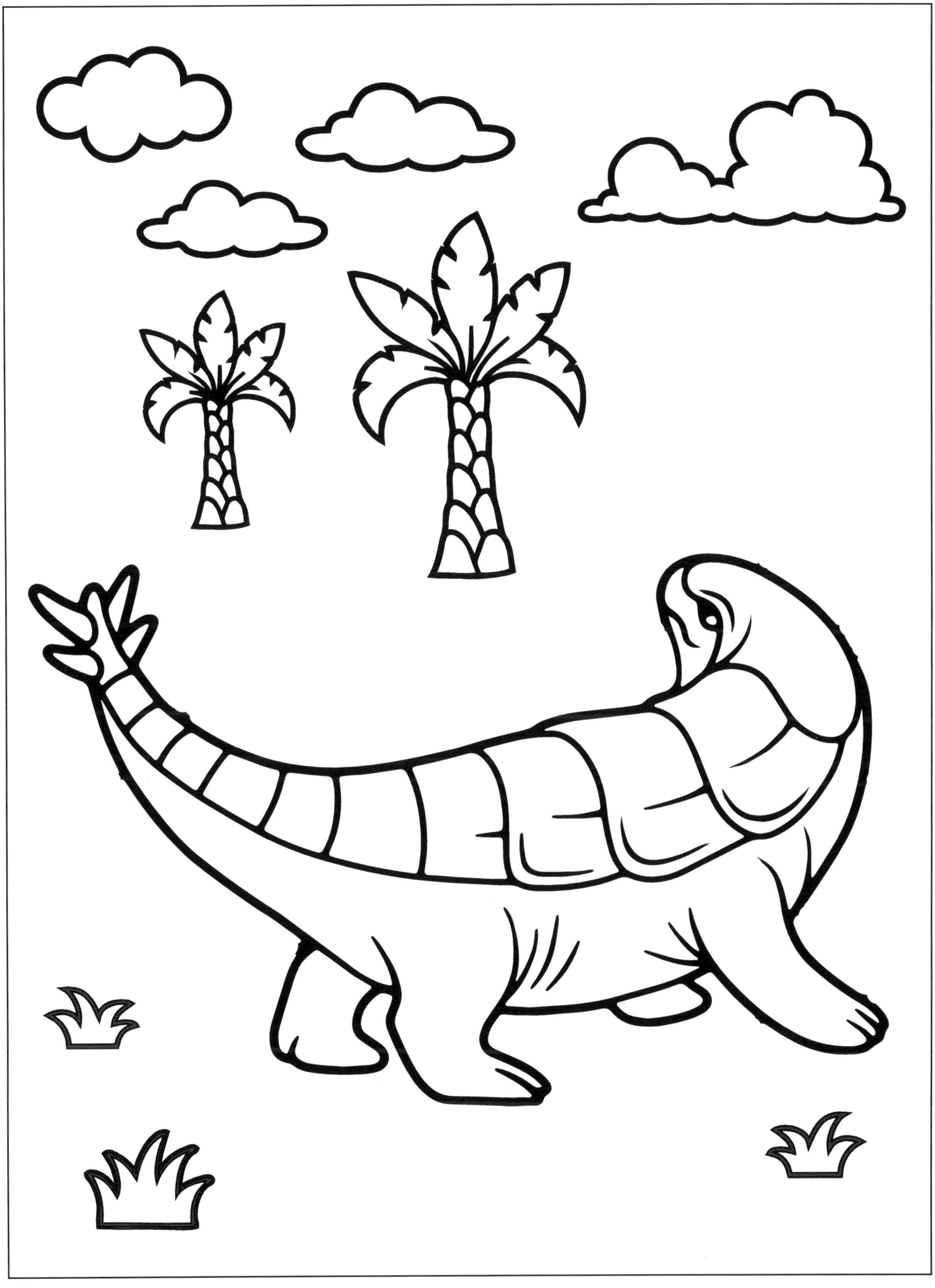

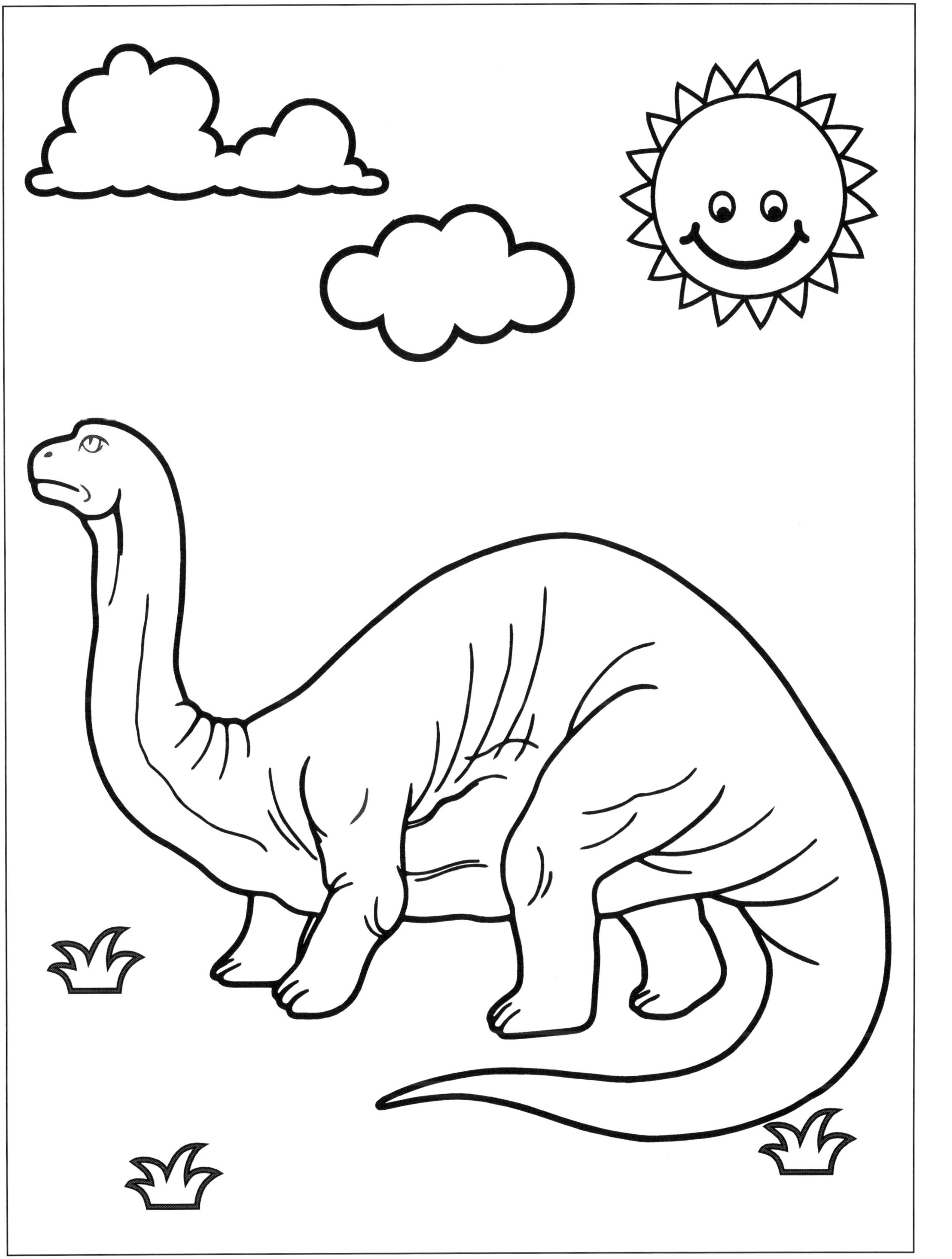

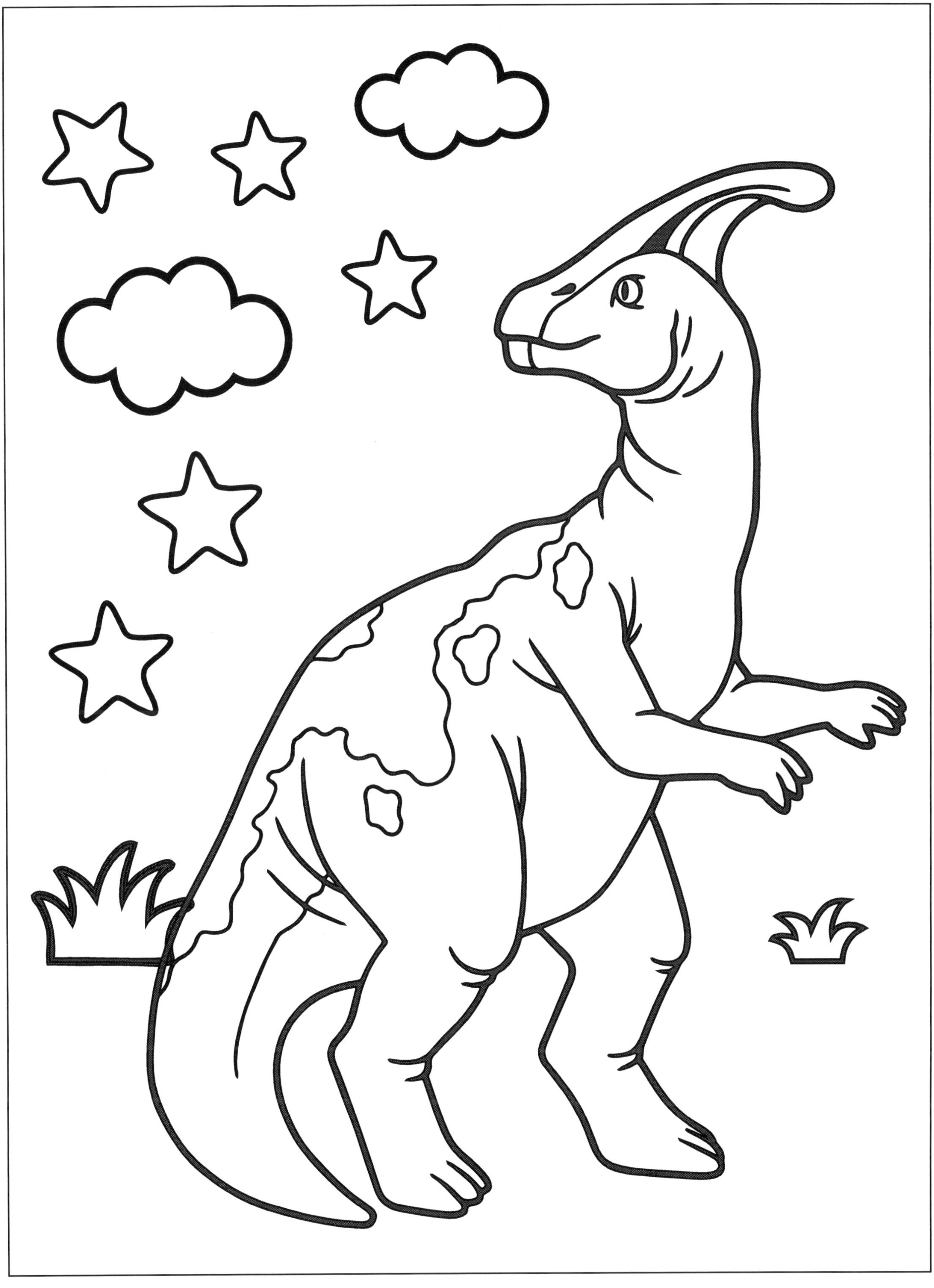

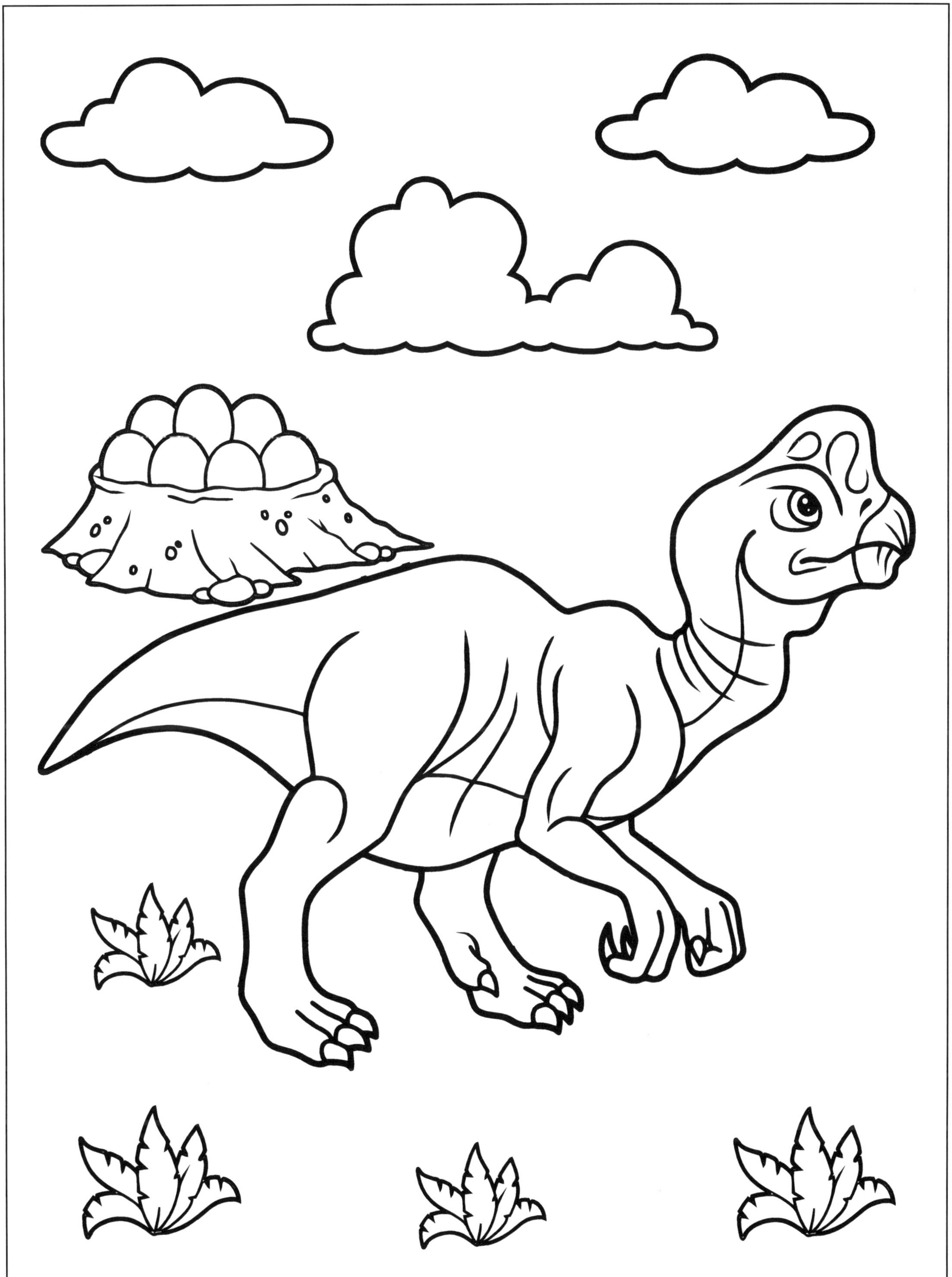

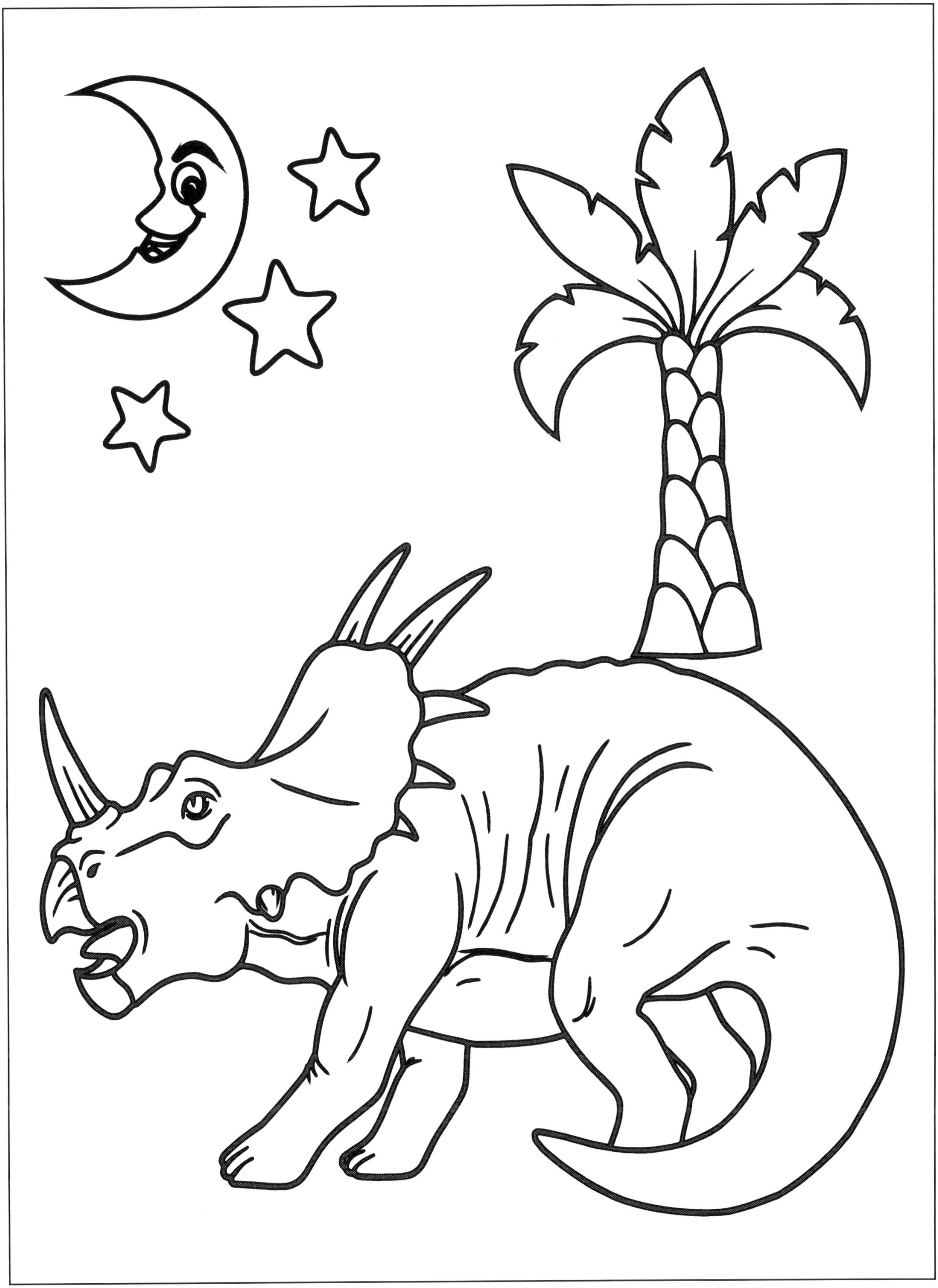

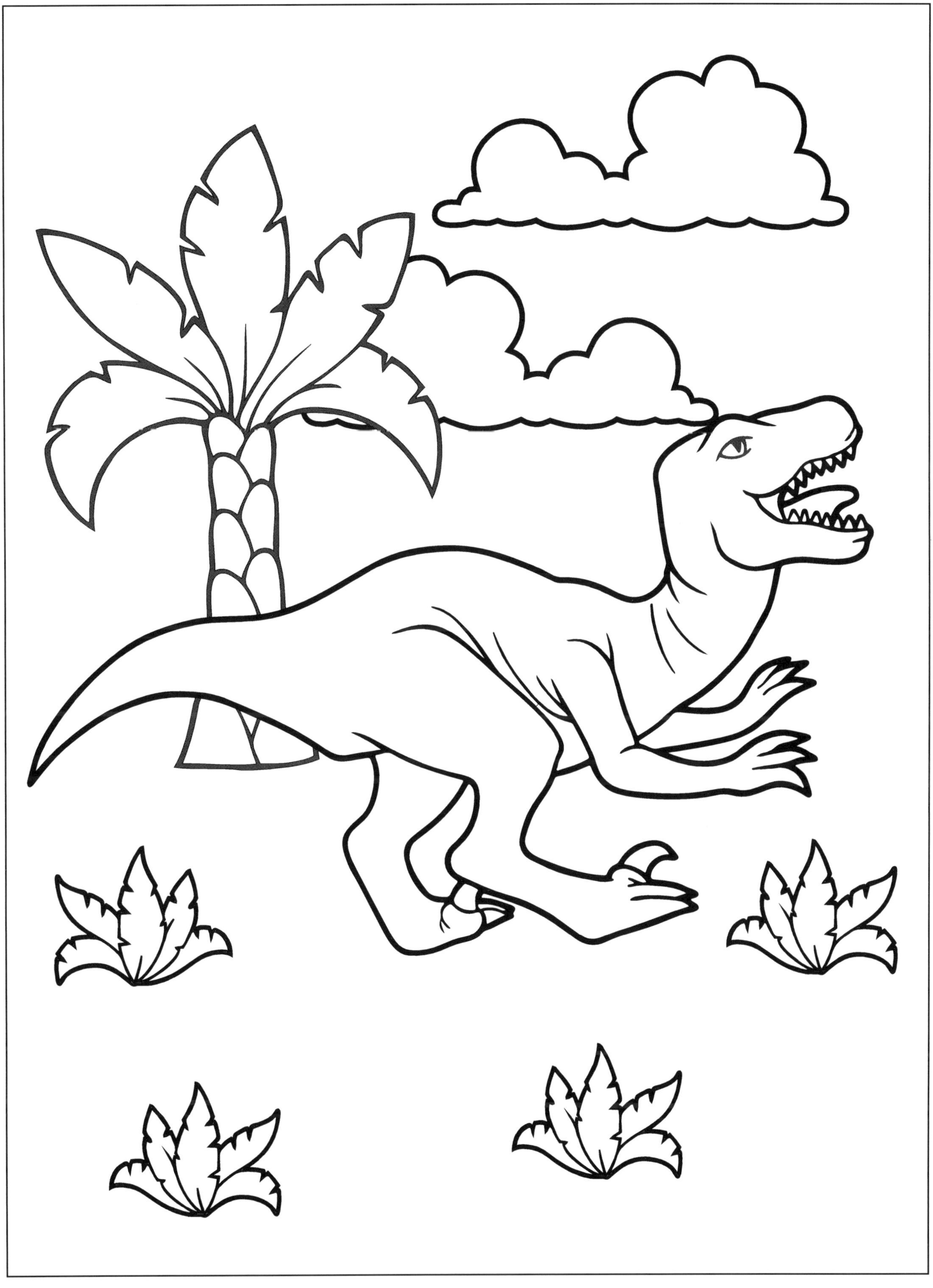

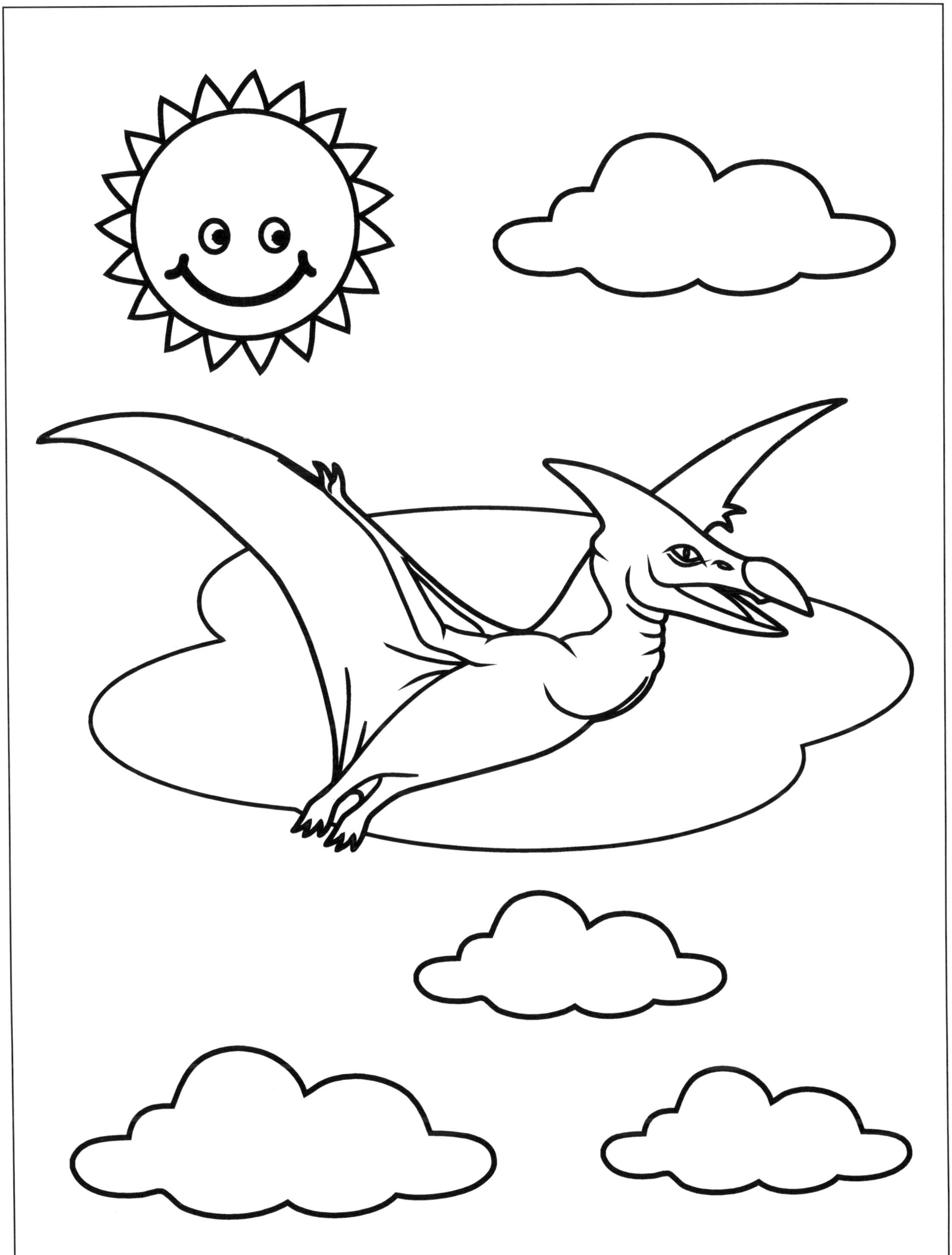

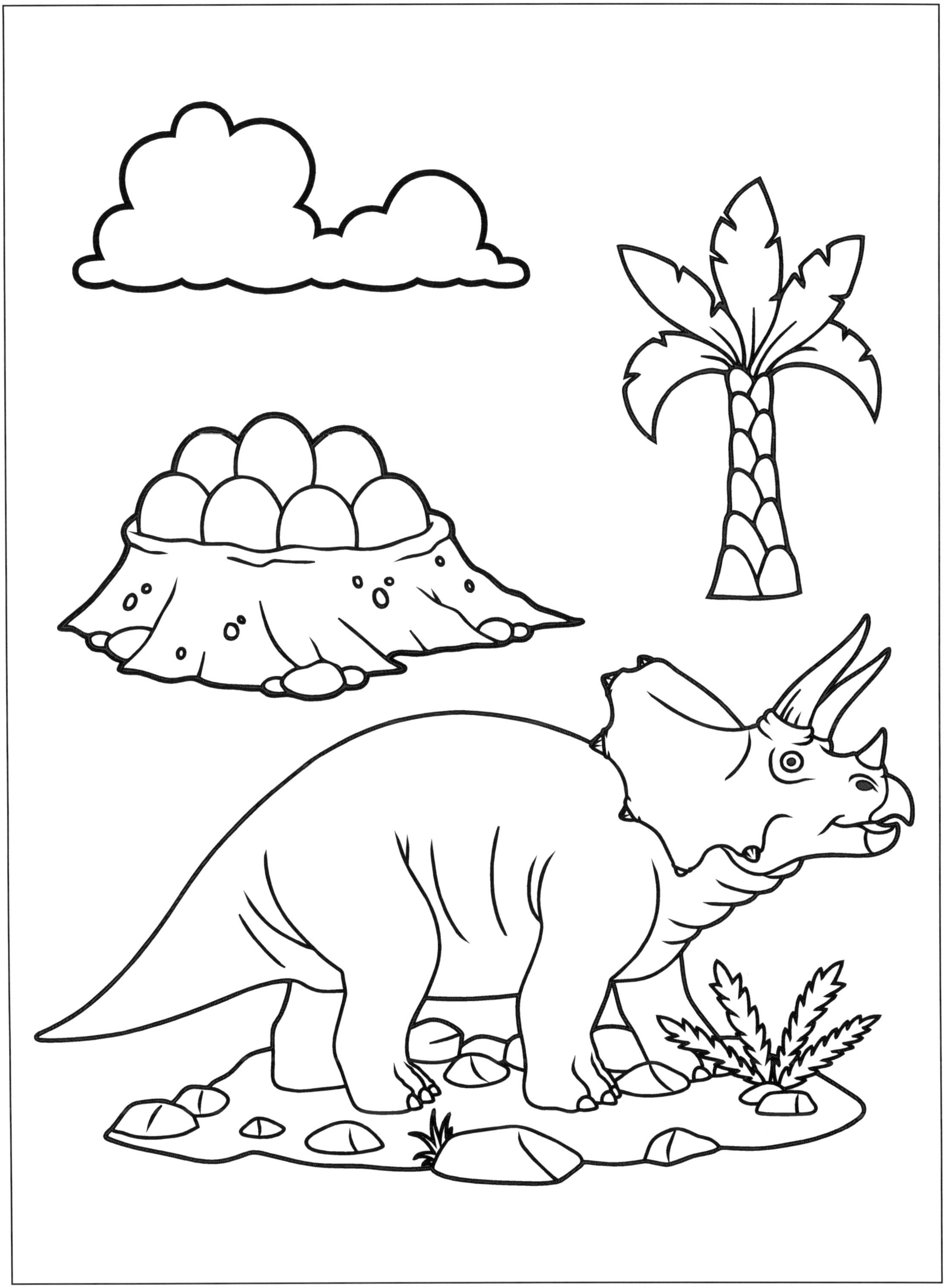

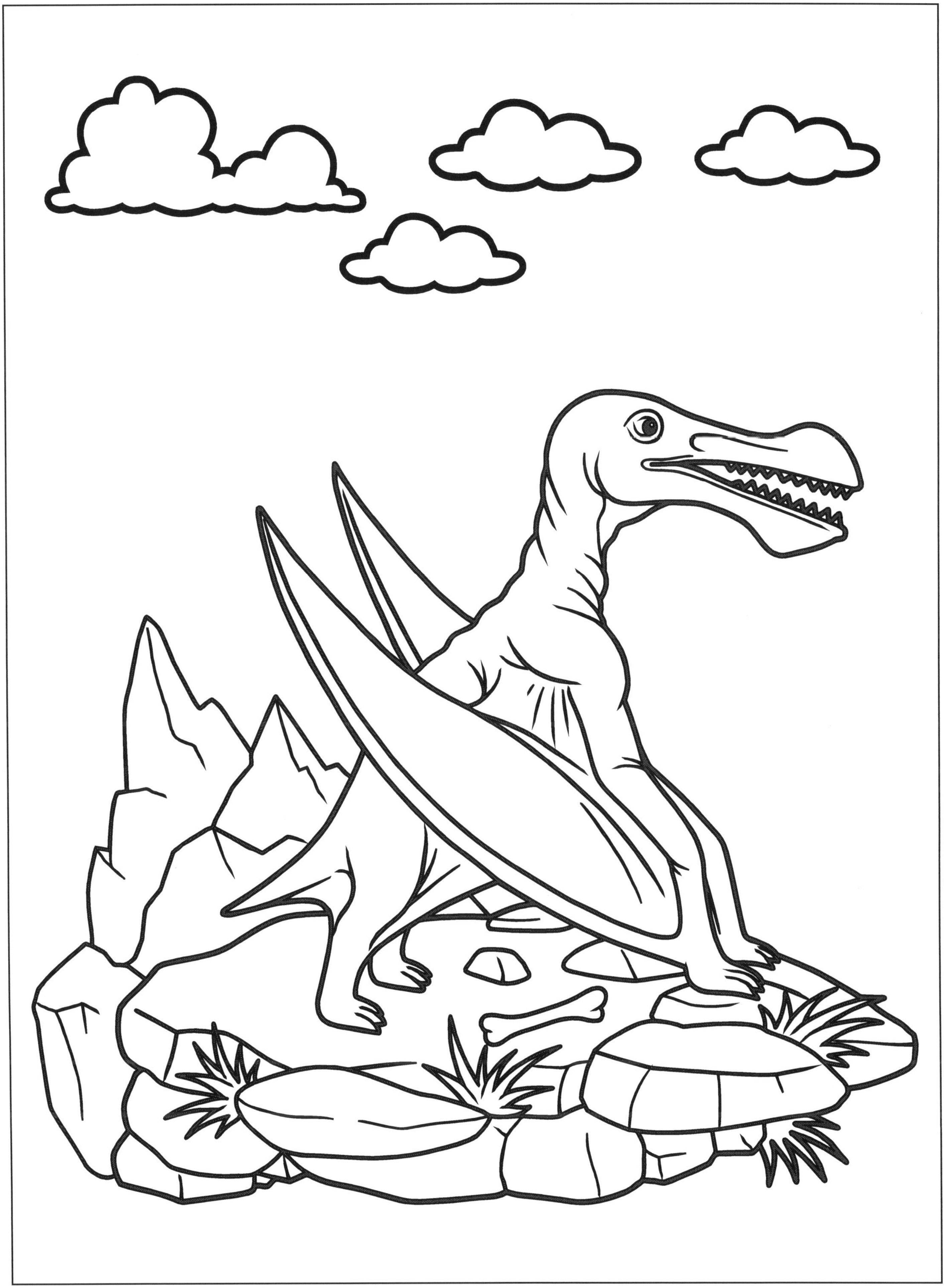

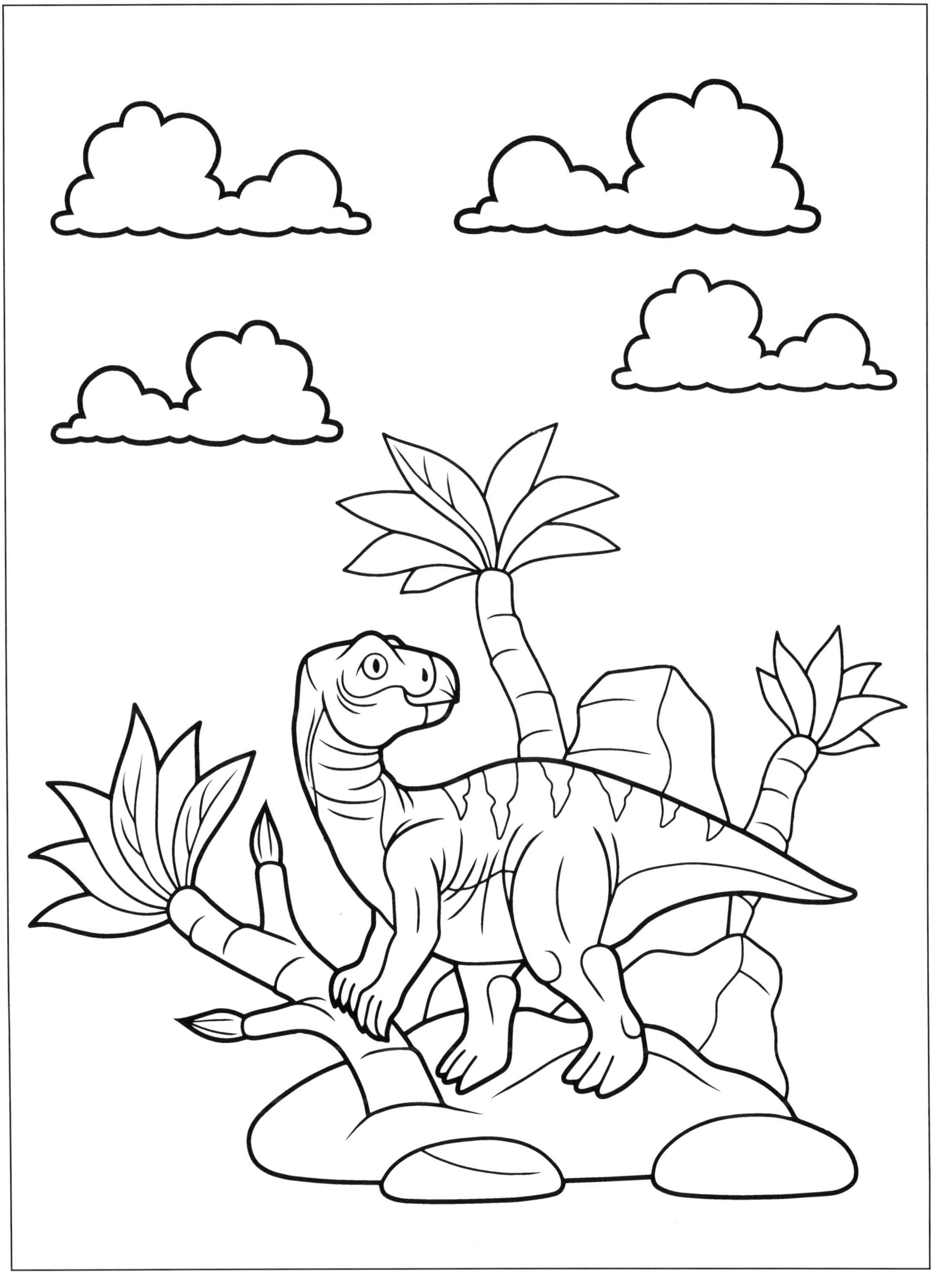

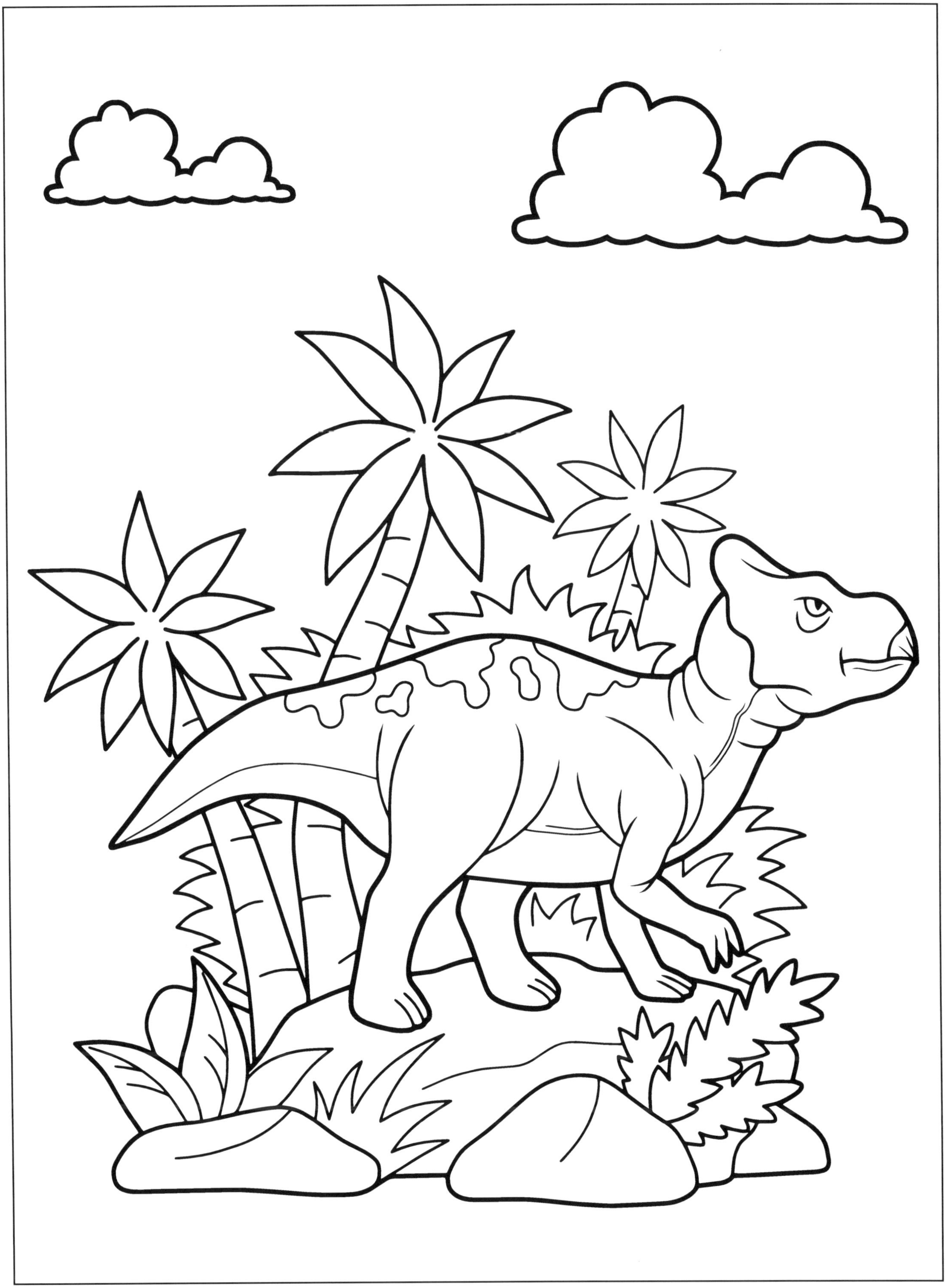

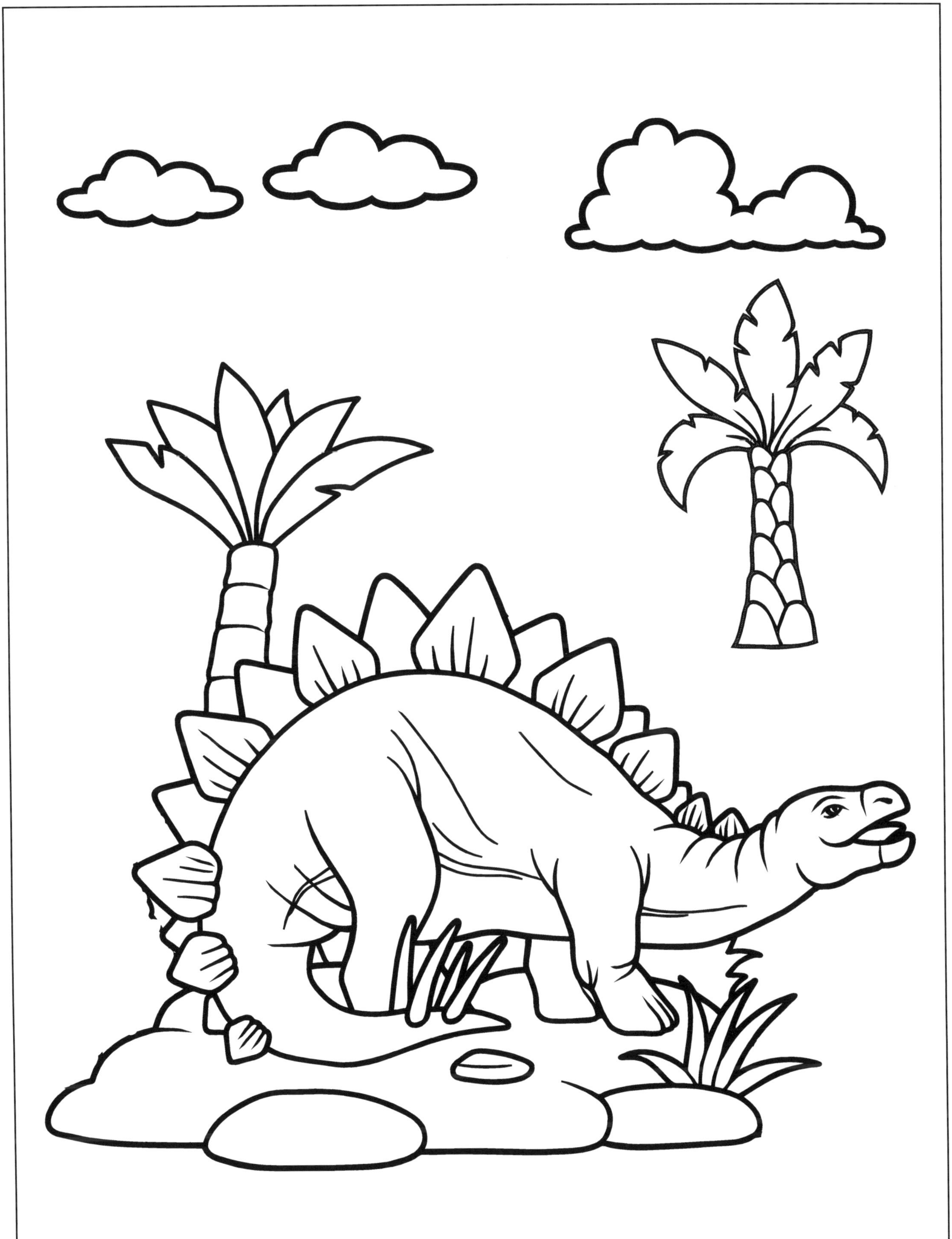

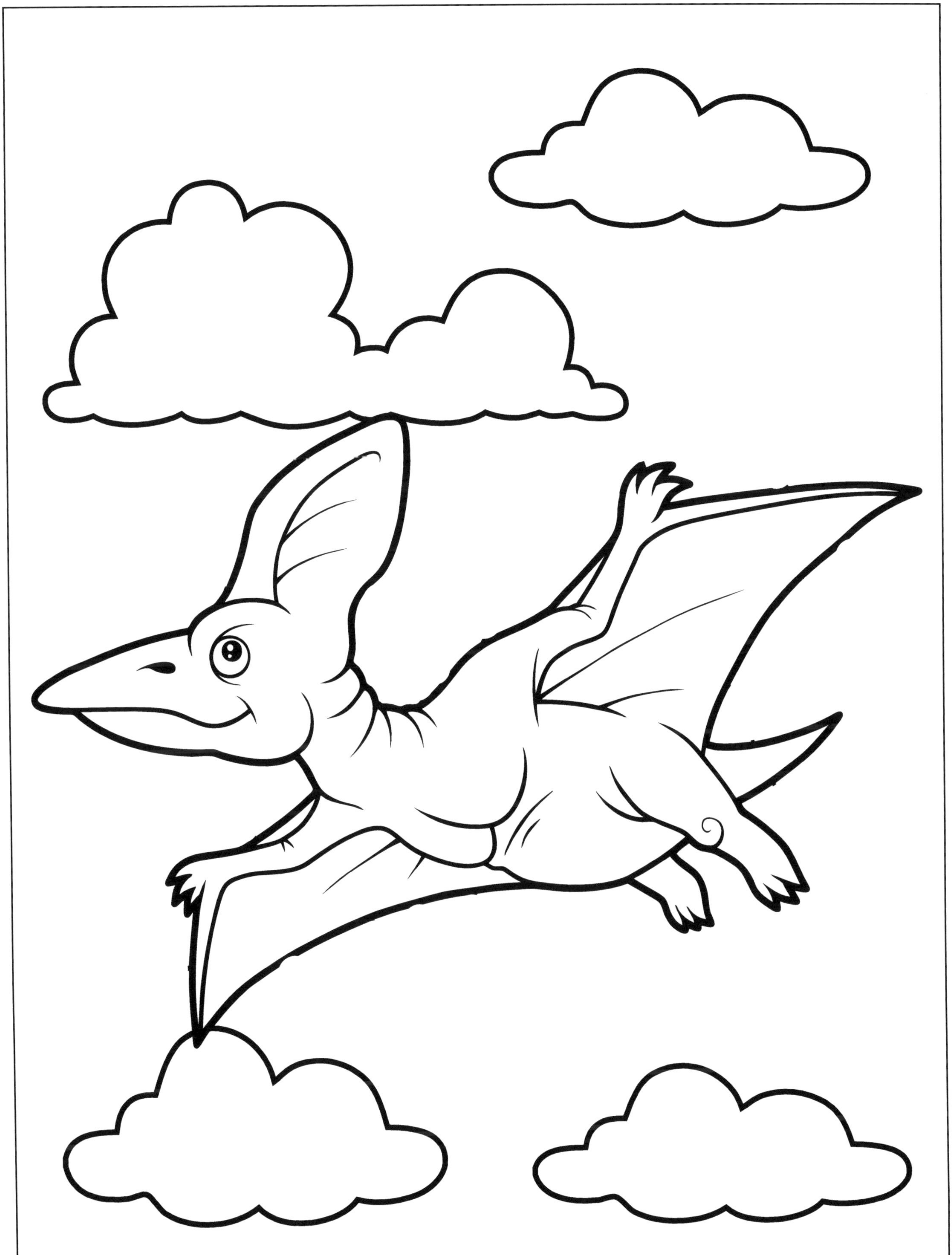

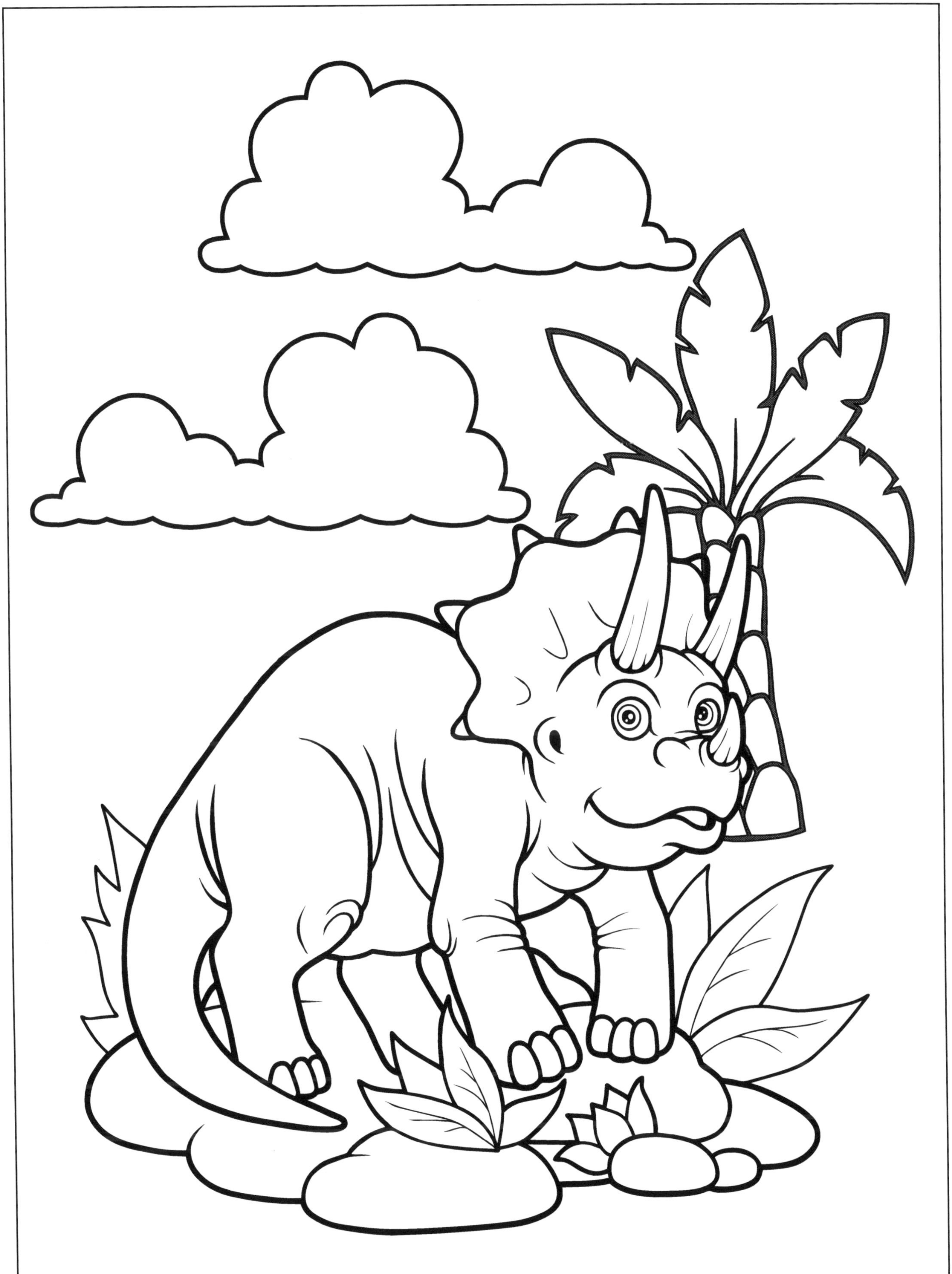

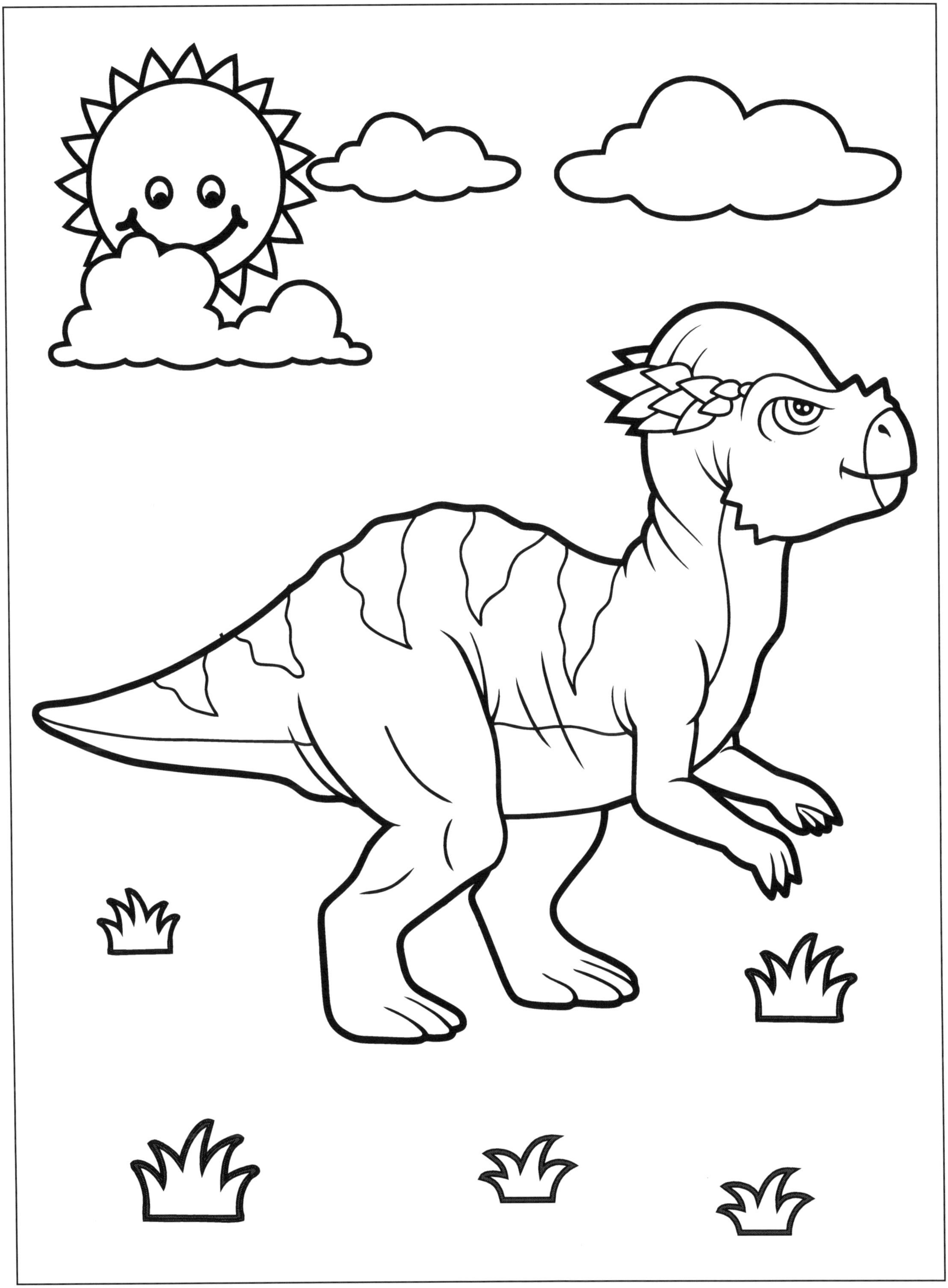

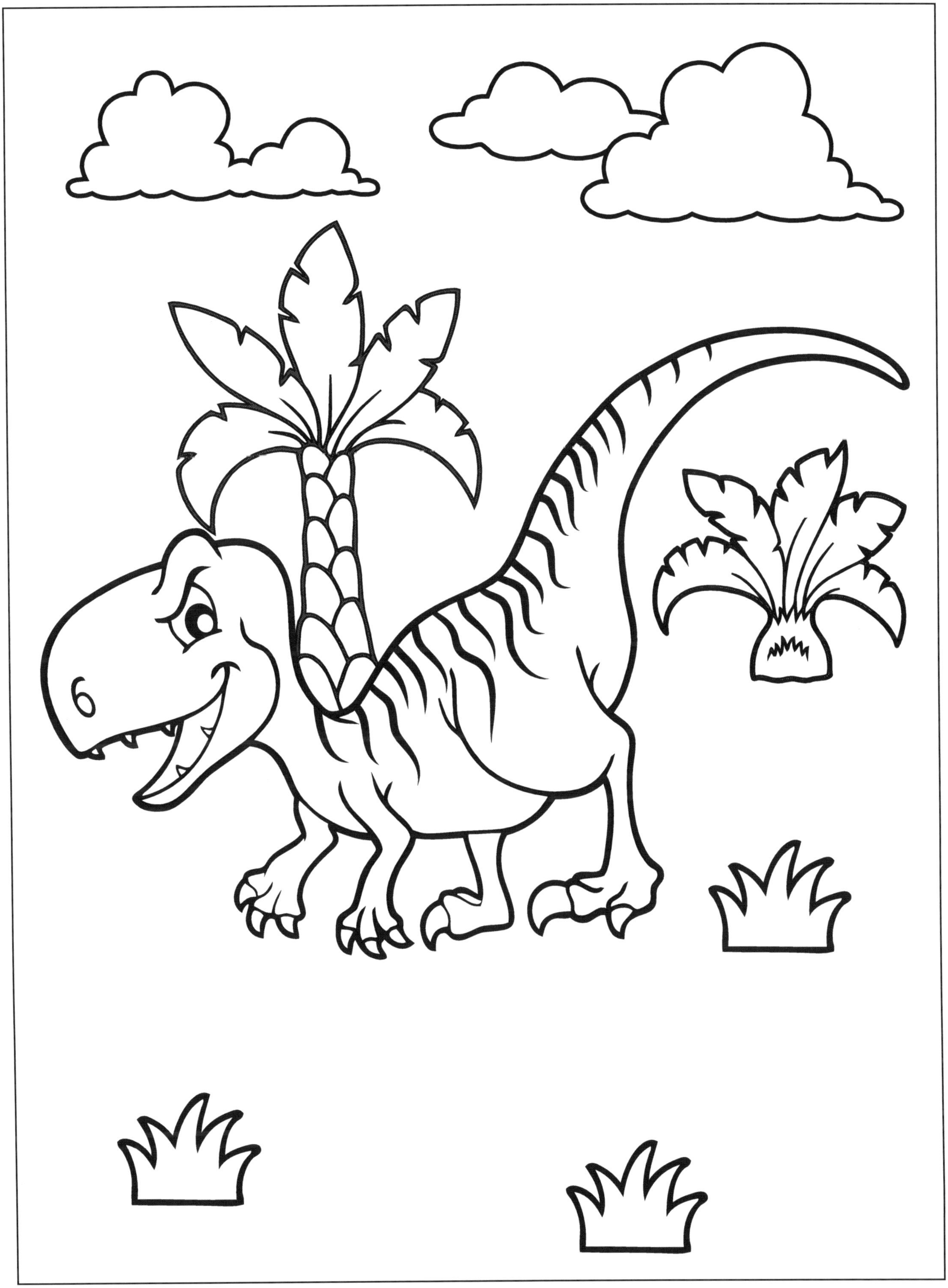

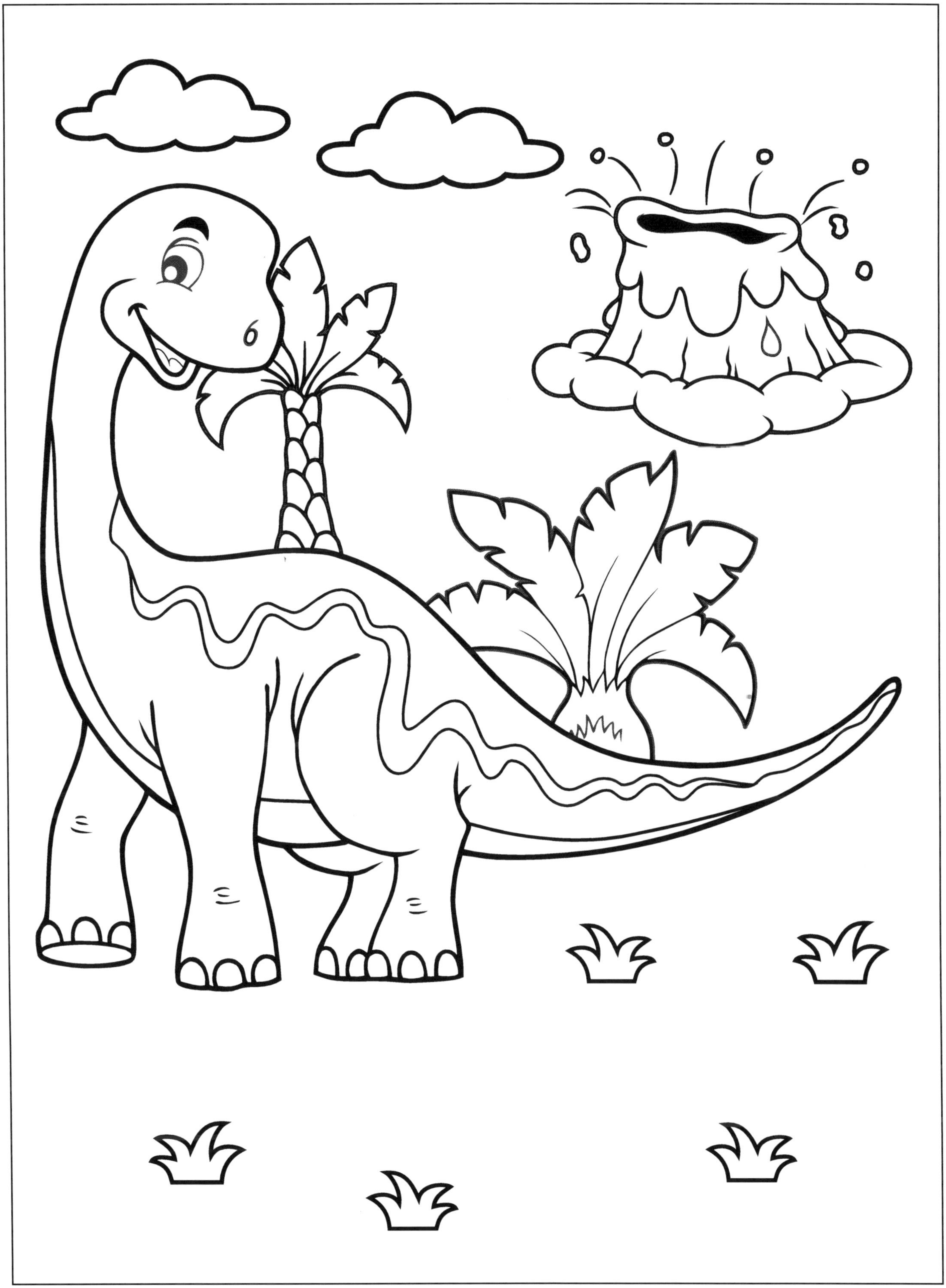

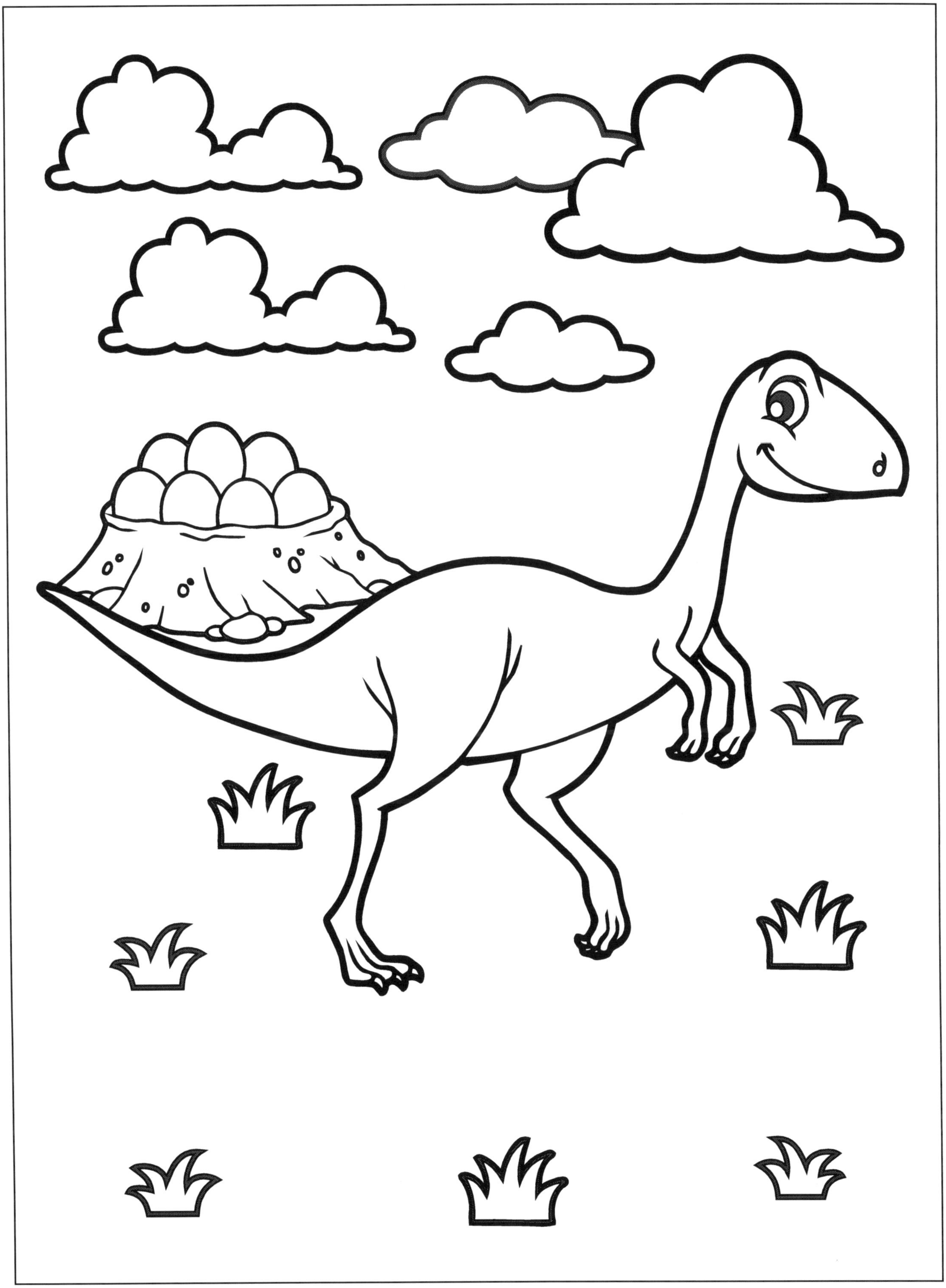

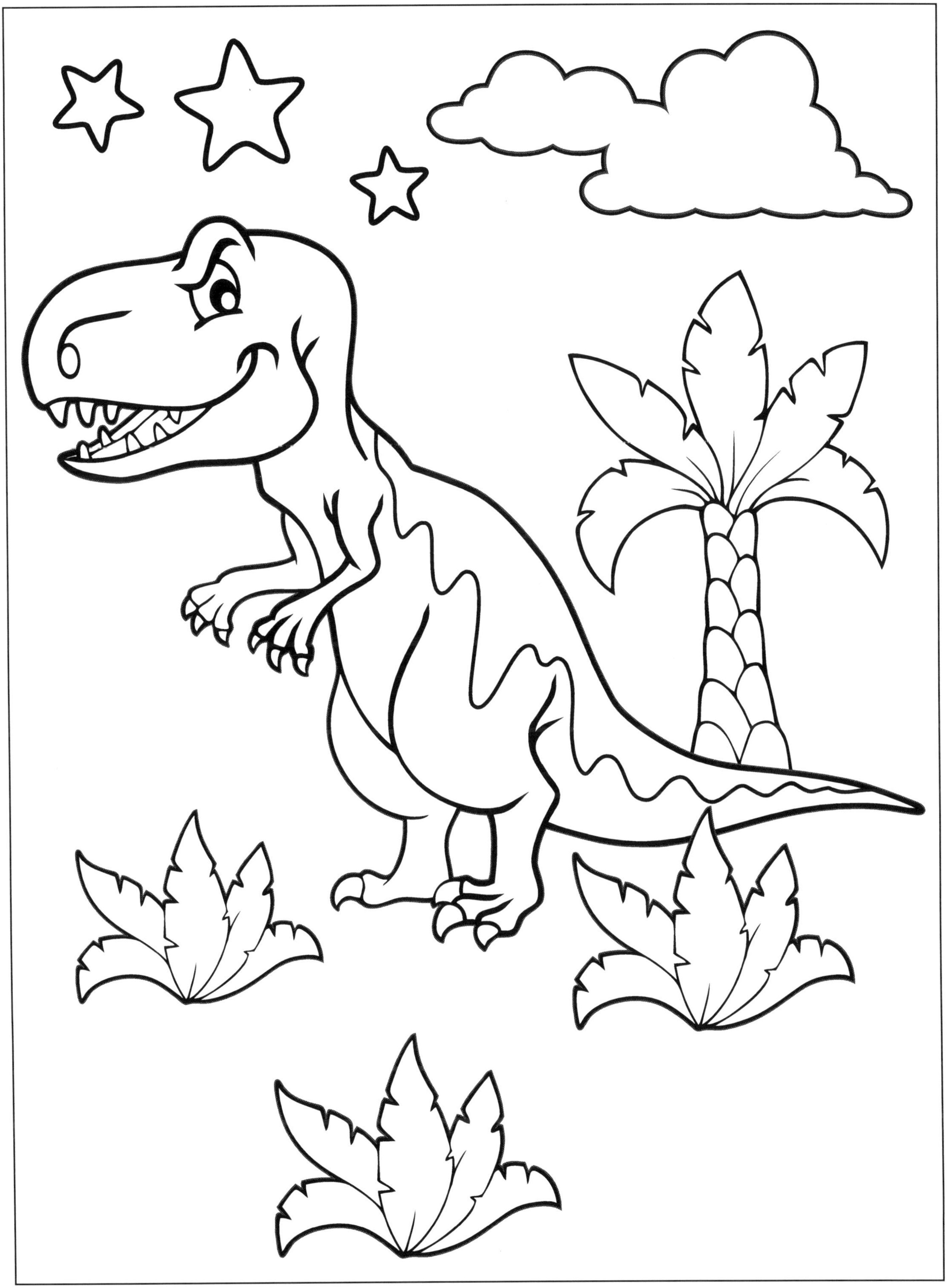

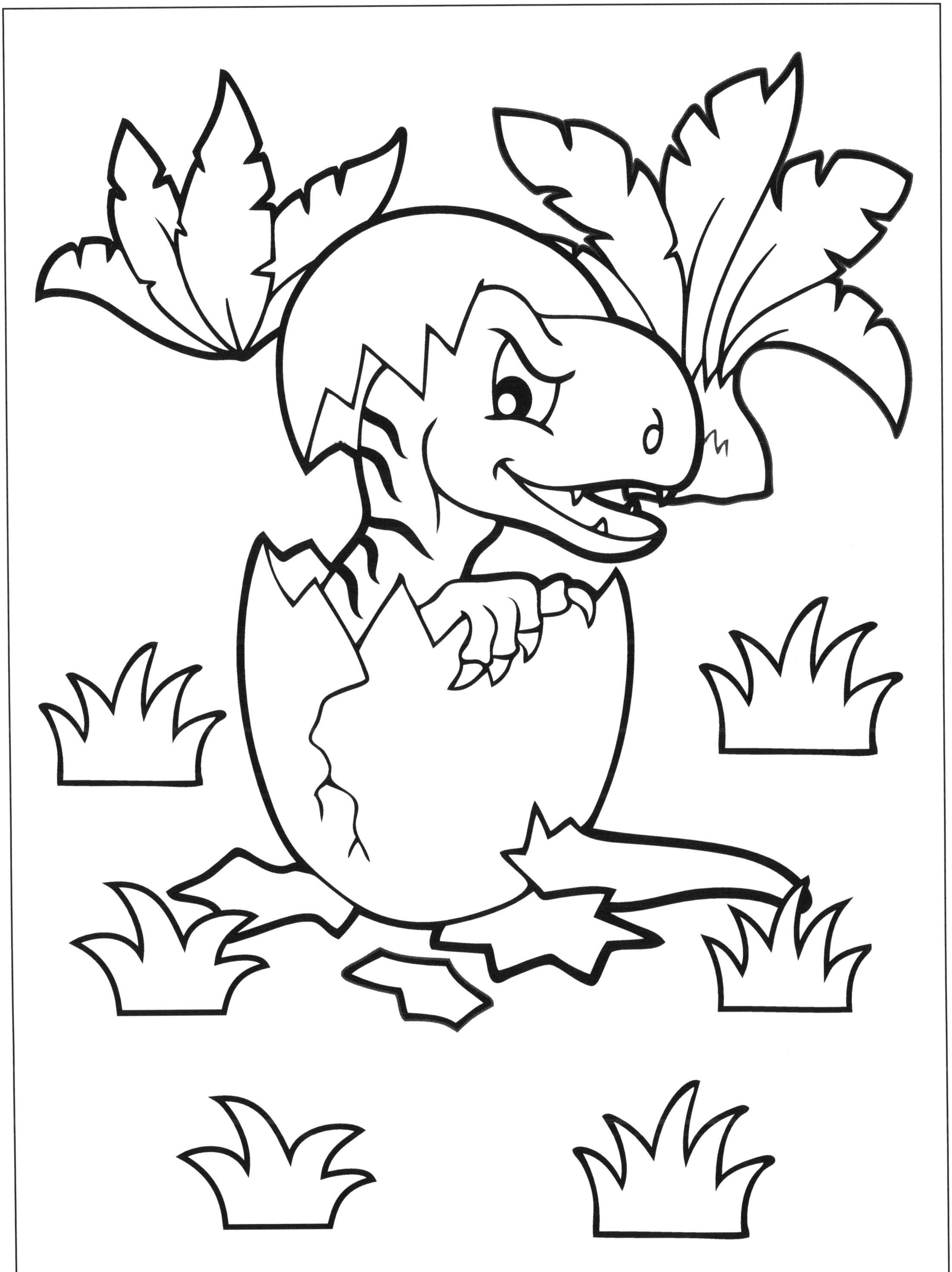

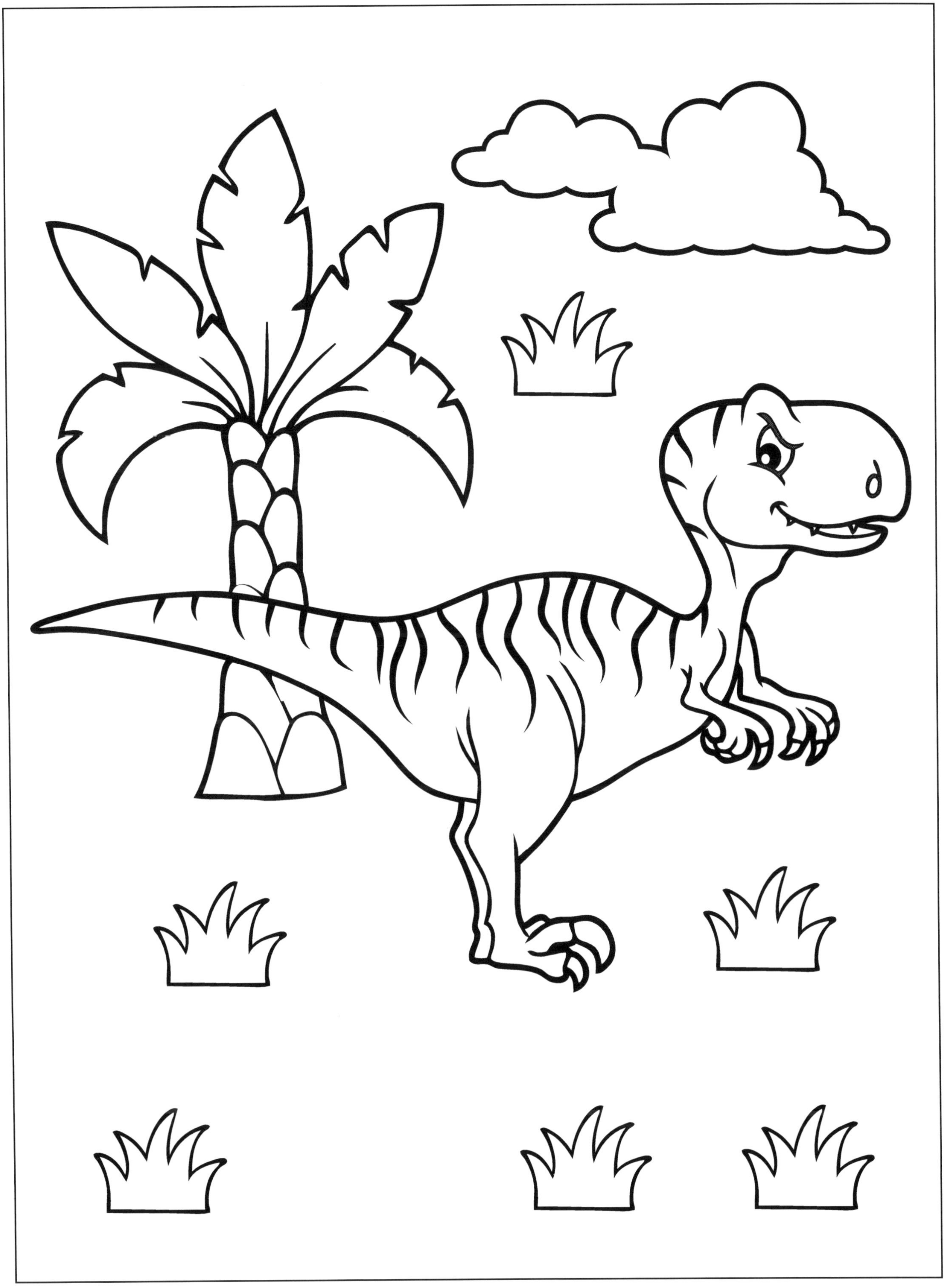

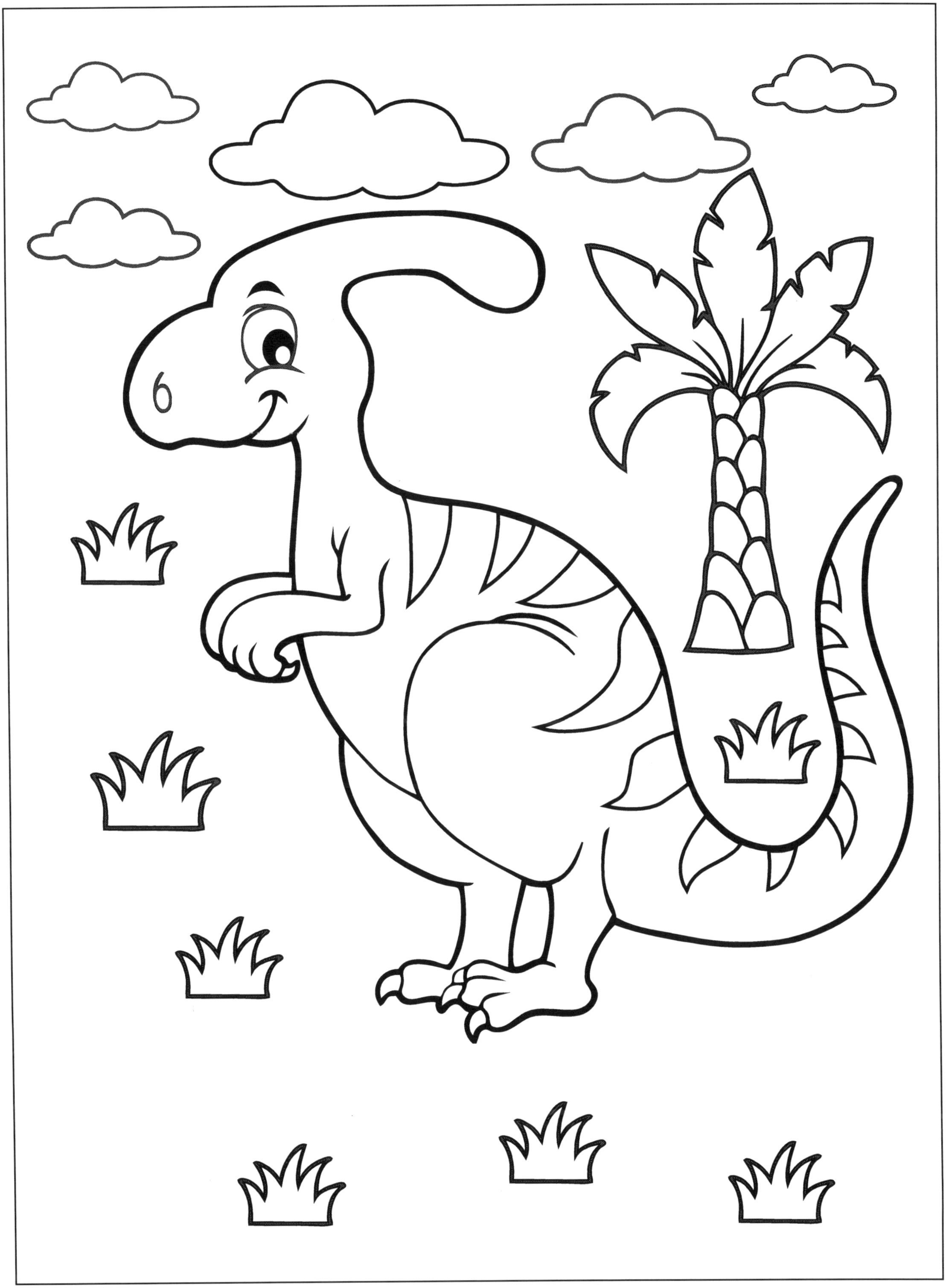

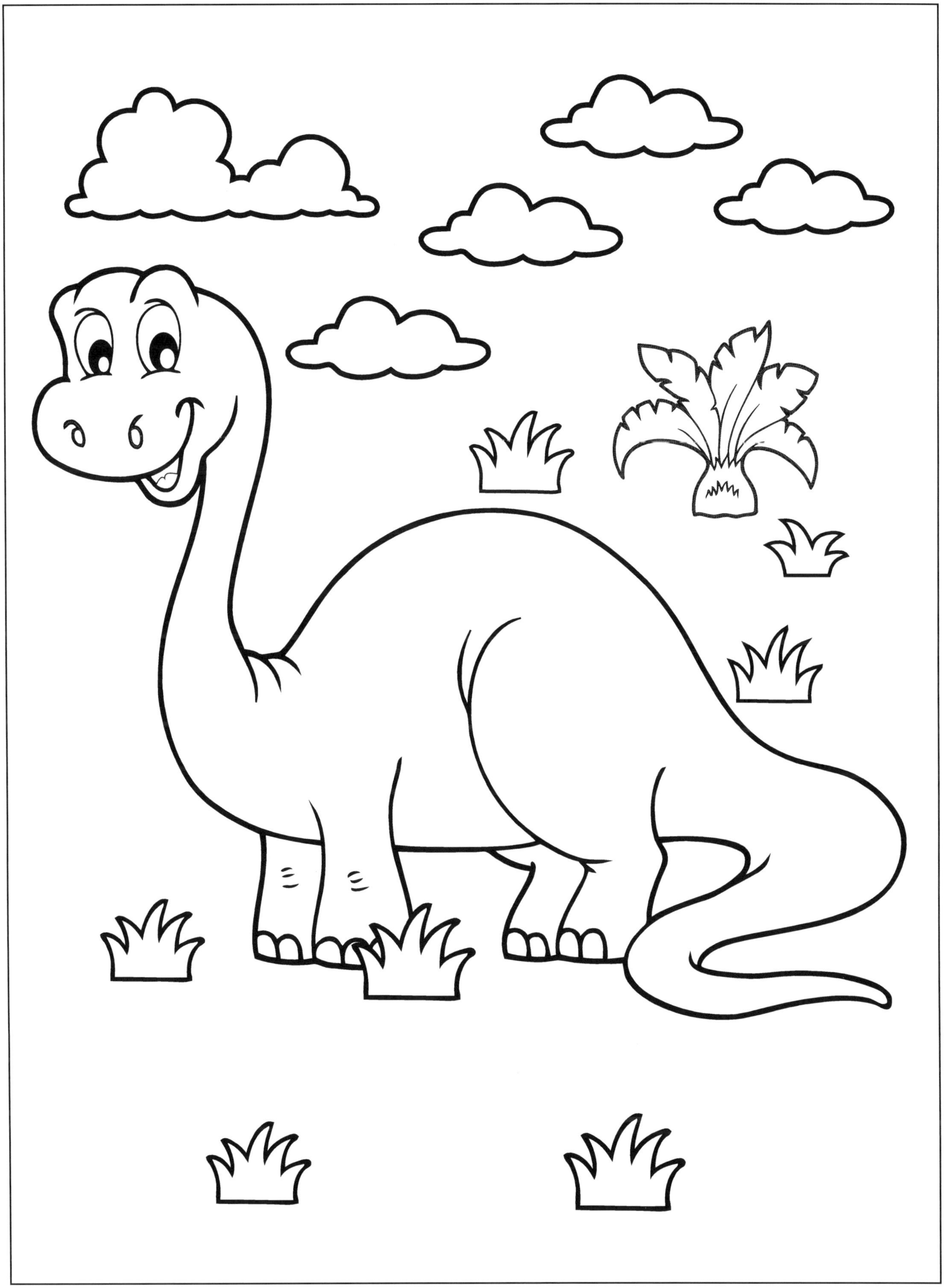

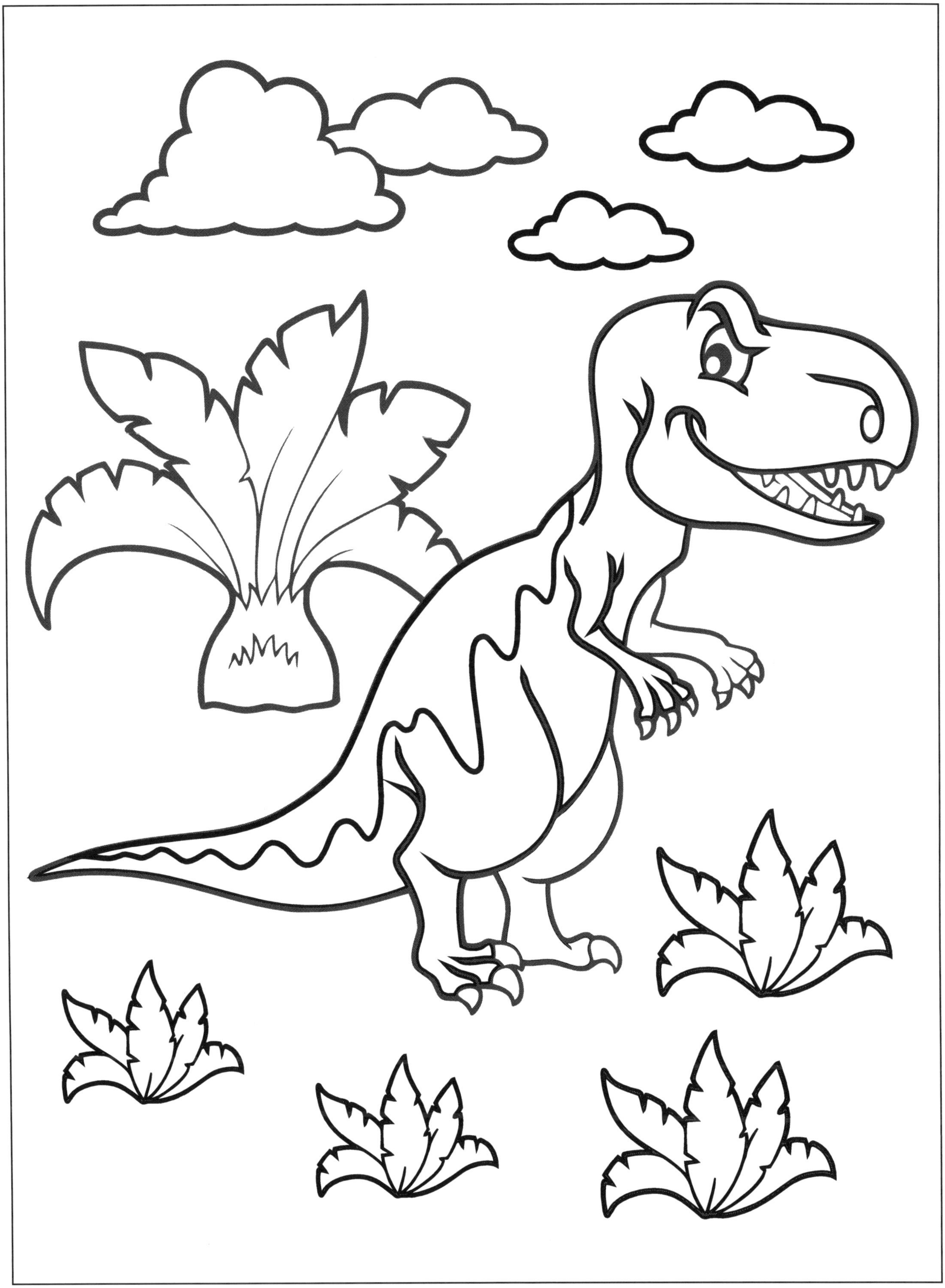

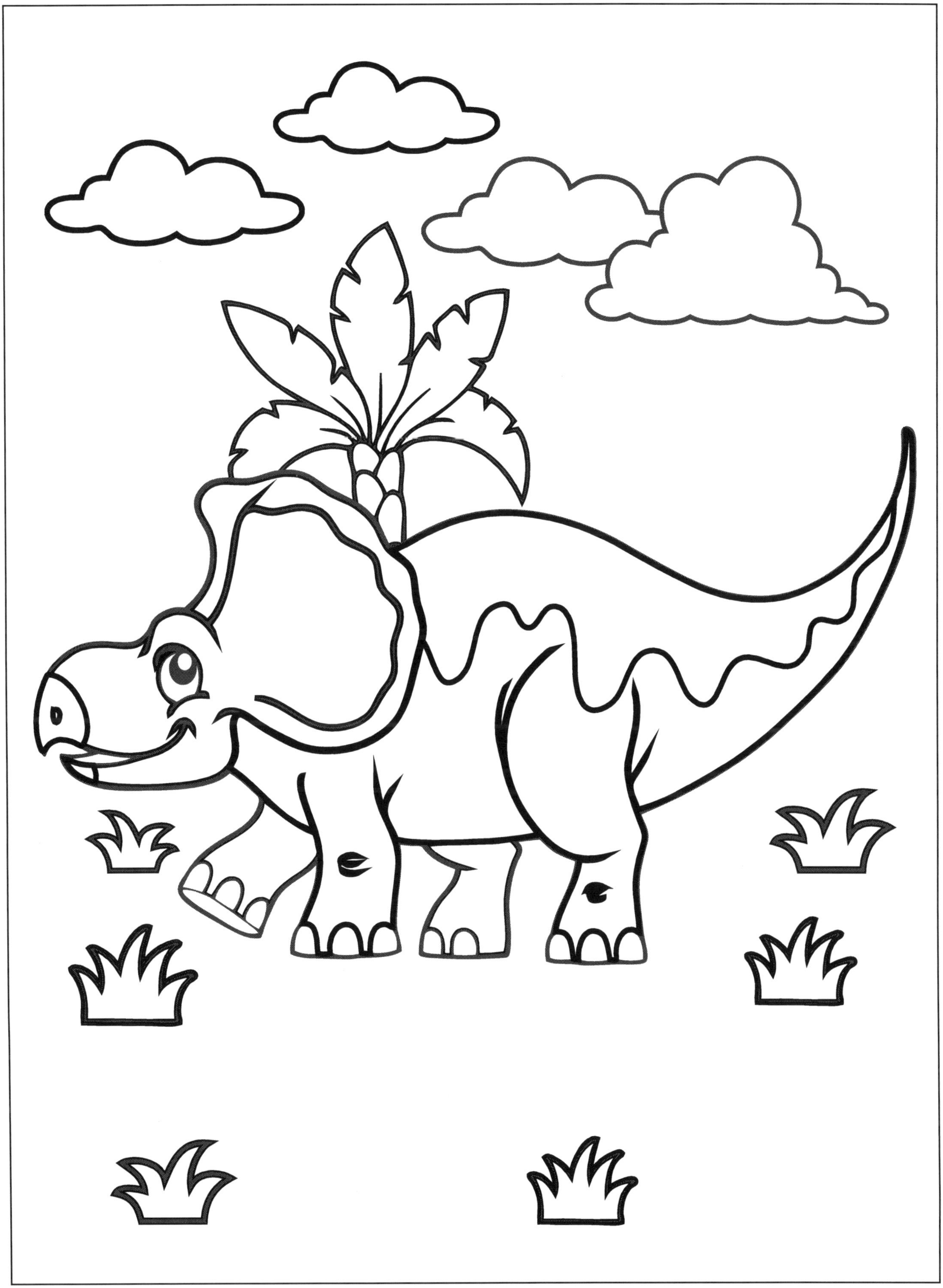

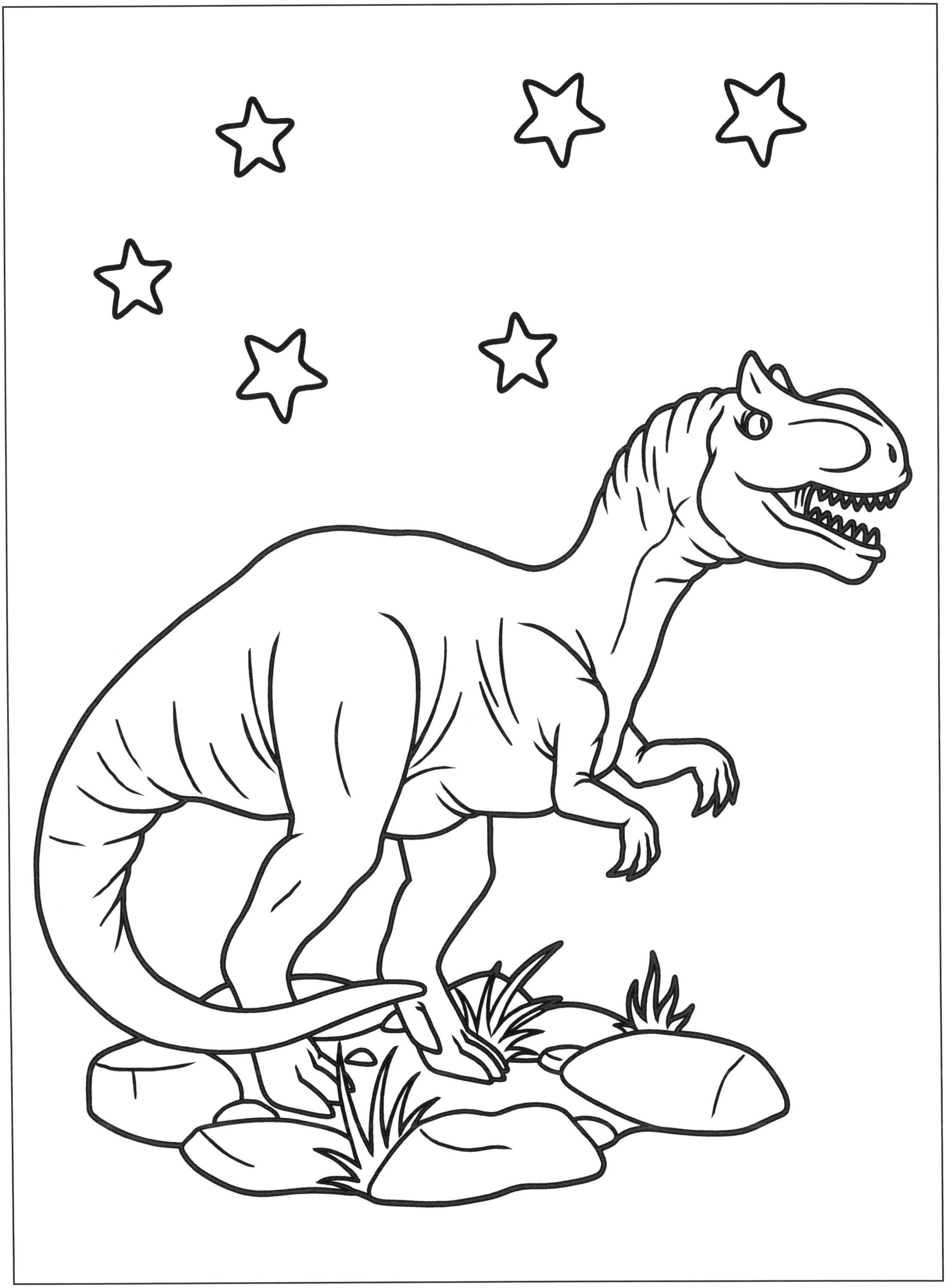

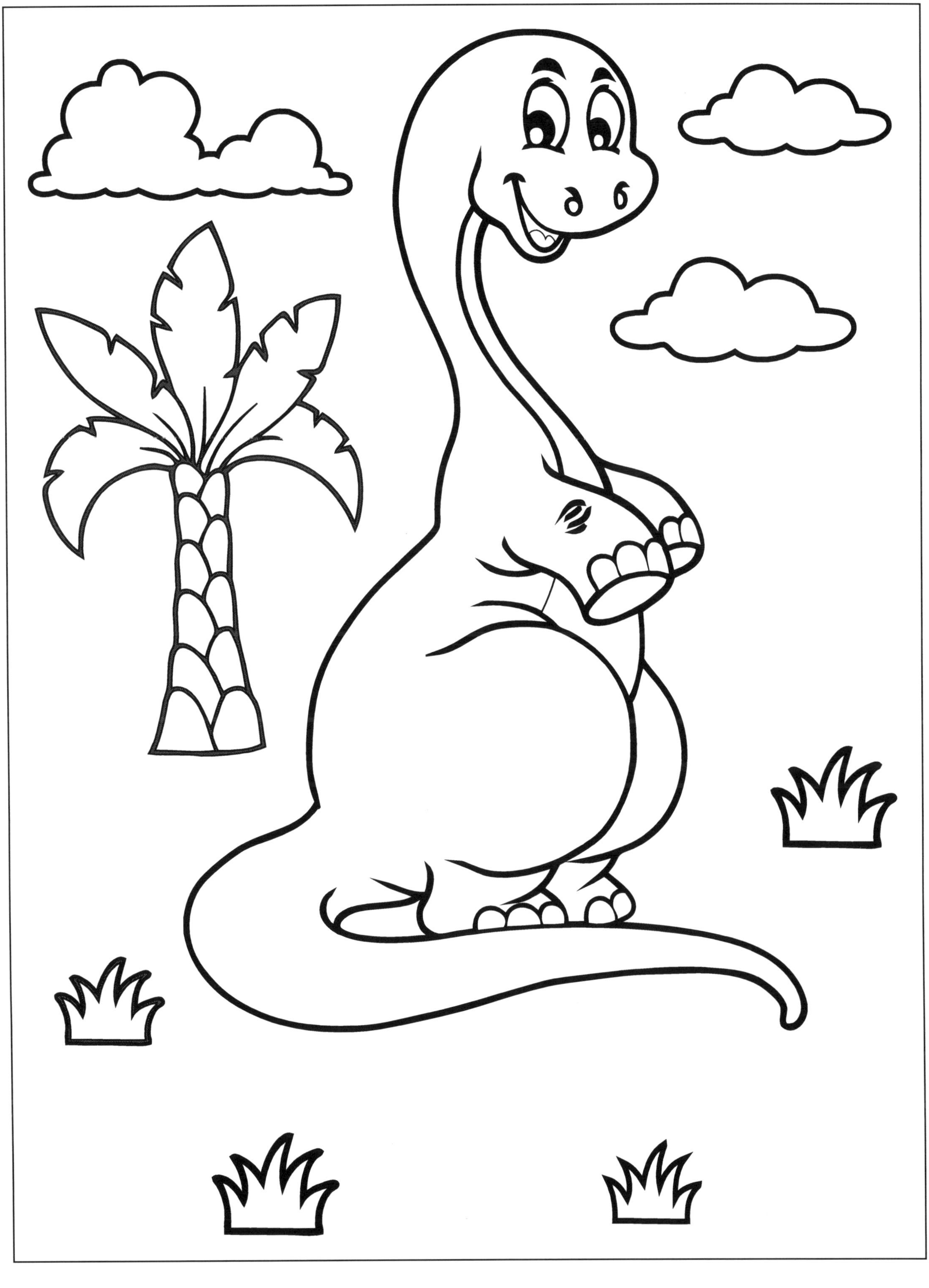

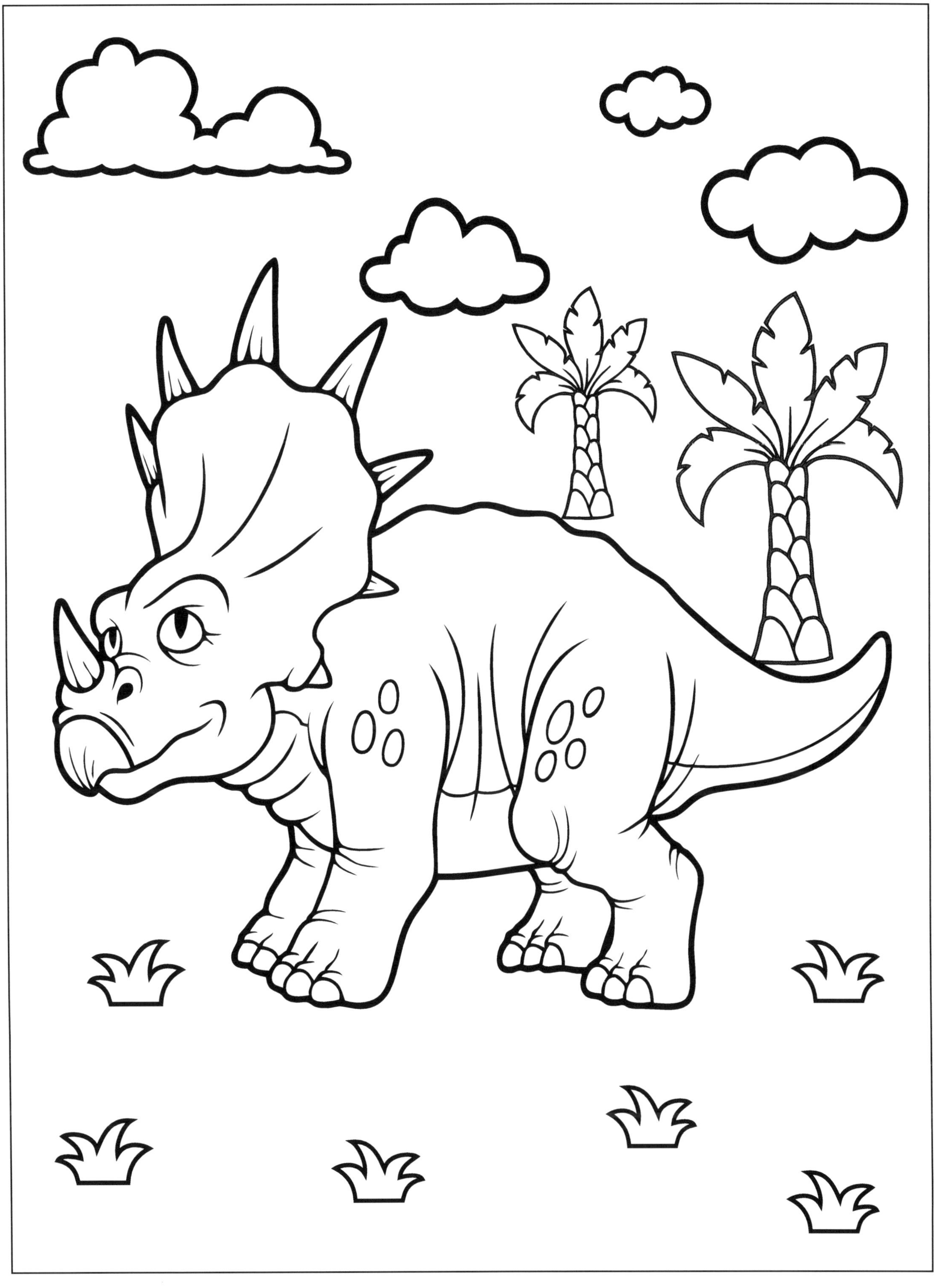

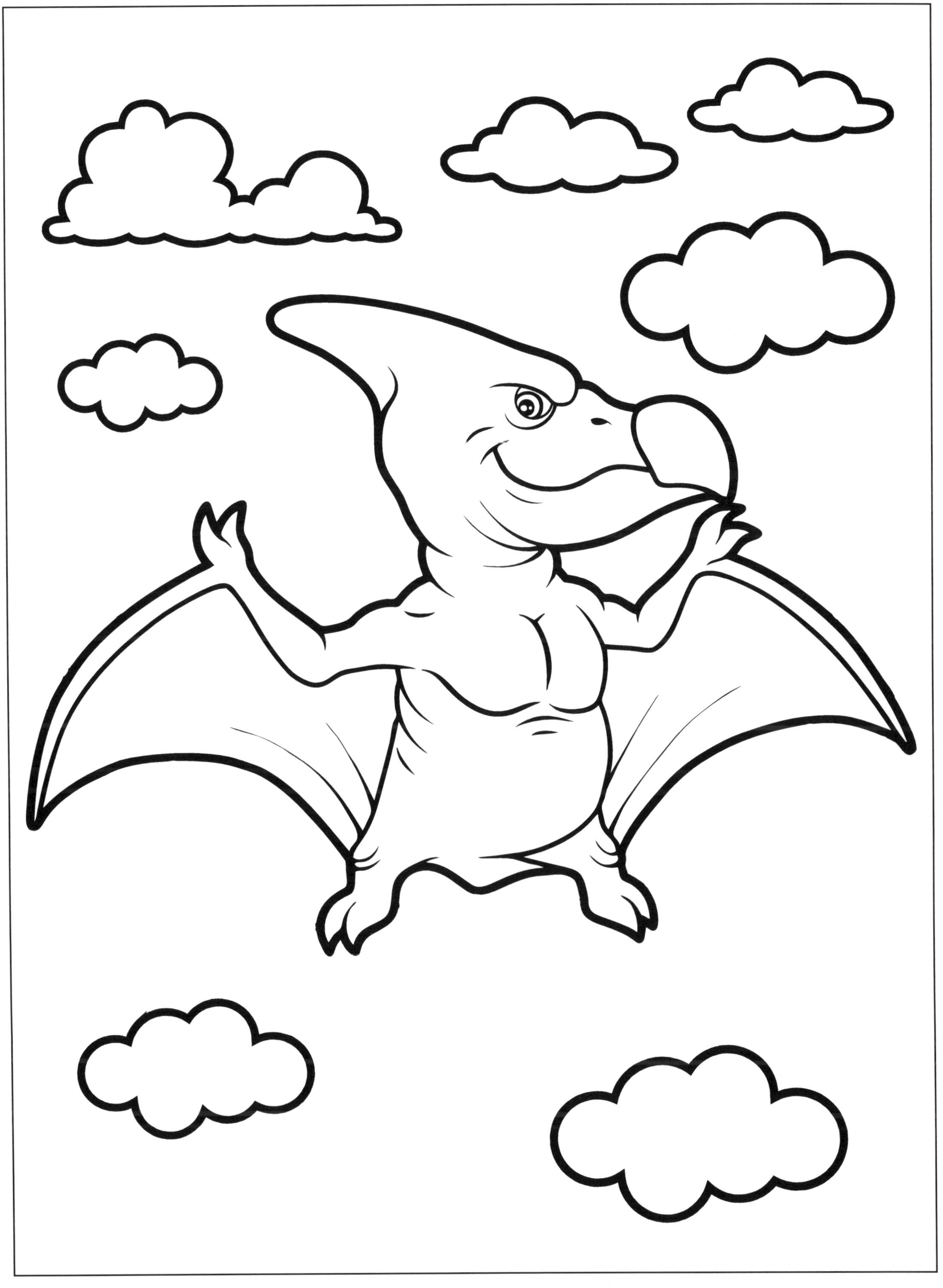

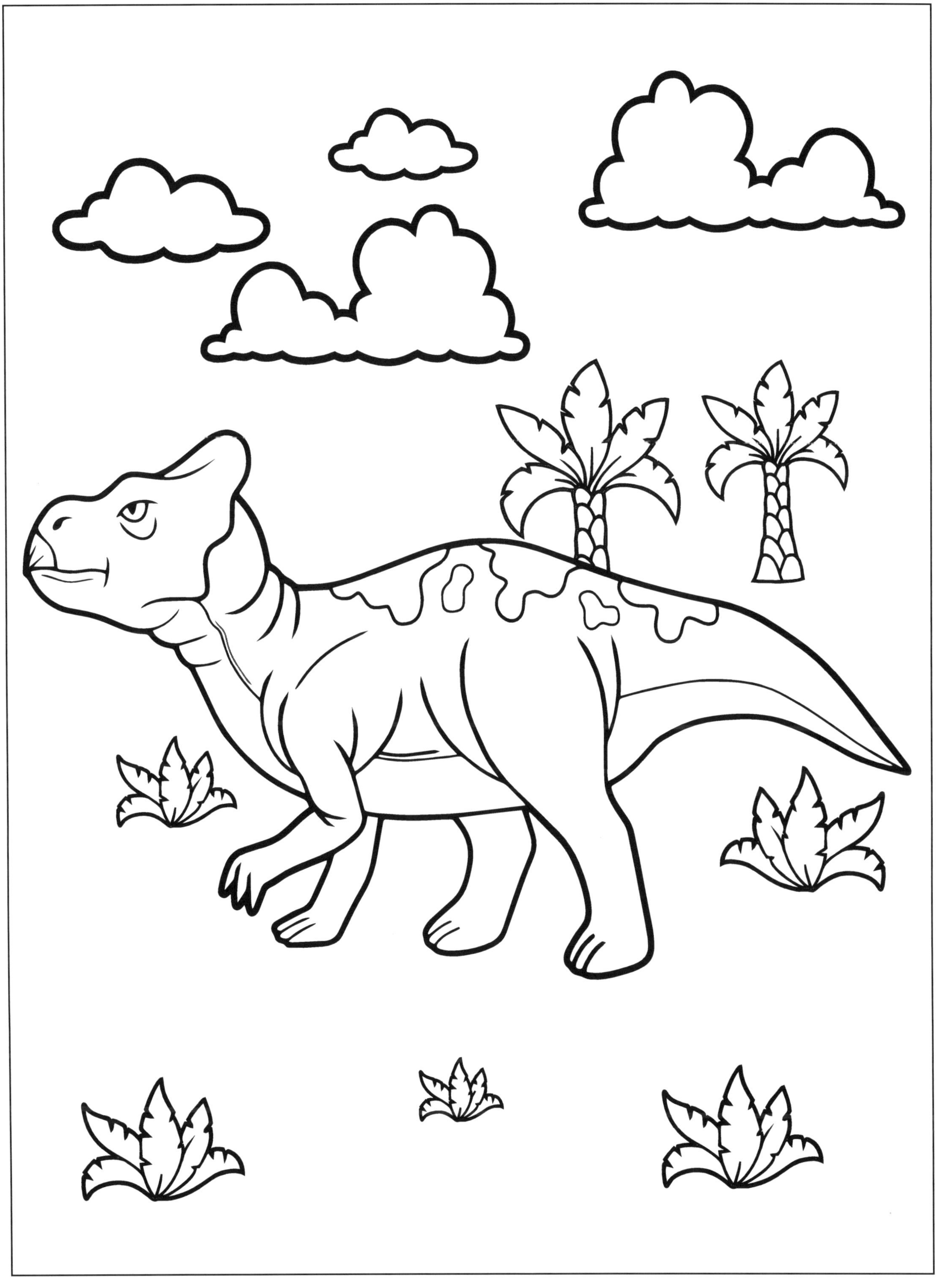

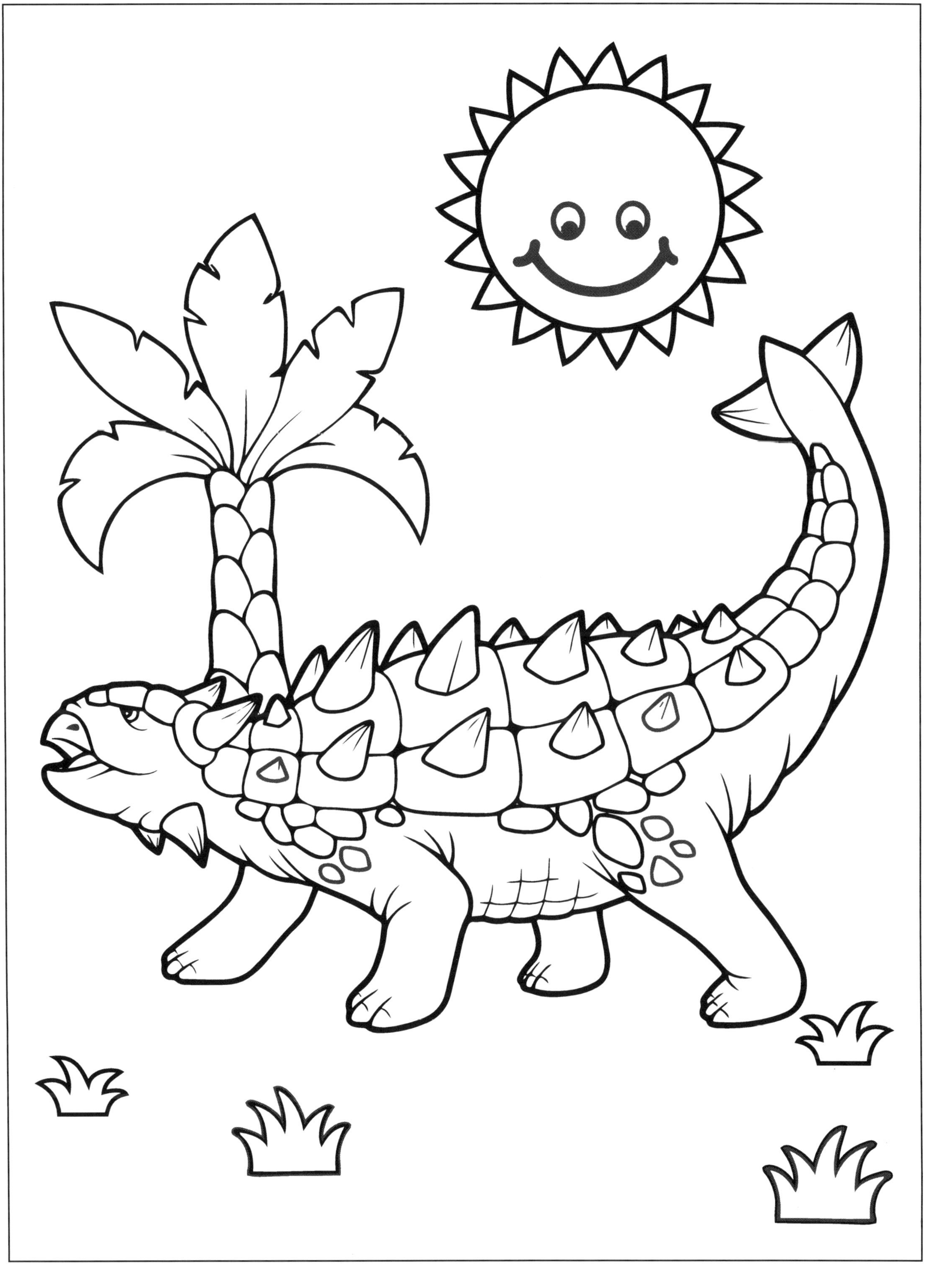

Source Images: Credit to - Fargon, Sarawut Padungkwan, Klara Viskova

47147639R00060

Made in the USA
Middletown, DE
17 August 2017